# The Reluctant
# Medium

# The Reluctant Medium

Reclaiming the Power of Women's Intuition

Lorri Ann Devlin, RN BSN MS

Printed in the United States of America
ISBN: 0692808442
ISBN 13: 9780692808443

Devlin, Lorri.
The Reluctant Medium / Lorri Devlin
ISBN 9780692808443

*To my teachers:*
*those who were imprisoned;*
*those who were ignored;*
*those who were burned, beaten, mocked, and shunned;*
*those who dared utter unpopular truths;*
*and those who kept silent,*
*surviving to share their misunderstood*
*gift with children of a wiser age.*

# Contents

The emergence of man, and the emergence of the human mind, may be seen as serving the evolutionary process...It is as if the processes of nature, evolution, and mind lead to the development of criteria consistent with evolutionary continuity. At one time before the parts were separated from the whole, nature, evolution, and mind were one and each arose out of an undifferentiated unity... Most human beings do not see themselves, or their minds, as serving the process of evolution. Nevertheless, it would represent a major phase change in the evolution of human consciousness for such a realization to occur and be acted upon. At this point in our evolution, as we further cultivate the human mind, we are becoming more and more aware of the role and the importance of intuition and reason in human evolution as well as in everyday life.

—JONAS SALK

# Preface

HAVE YOU EVER known something you had no logical way of knowing? Perhaps it was a premonition—a realization or a vivid dream that stuck with you all day long and later came true. Do you have dreams that seem more real than "real" life? Do they feature a visit with a departed loved one?

If you're lucky, you have someone in your life with whom to share these things. Fear of being judged, labeled as crazy, or dismissed as a fool keeps many women with intuitive experiences silent.

I'm guessing you're a rational human being who's earned the respect of friends, family, and coworkers. You're intelligent and dependable, an expert in your particular field of work. But you're not comfortable talking about premonitions, intuition, and psychic awareness. If you have personal experience with metaphysical matters or know someone who has, you may not know how to integrate these irrational experiences into your everyday mind-set.

It's also possible you've never had a psychic experience but that you're curious. You suspect there's more to it than trickery and superstition. Well, whether you're familiar with the paranormal or just curious, welcome. We're going to explore the subject of psychic awareness and why it's critical to nurture your extraordinary, undervalued, and very real ability.

I'm a registered nurse. I'm a rational-health practitioner with a solid career. I'm a wife, author, and entrepreneur, with two grown-up sons who don't find me any more embarrassing than the typical parent. I'm also a person who's had psychic experiences since I was a little girl. I hear, and see, spirits. I have premonitions—I know things before they happen. I'm a medium, which means I'm able to sense and communicate with the departed. For most of my life, I lived in terrific fear of my abilities and hid them from all but my immediate family.

I'm visited by departed loved ones in dreams. I've seen a few ghosts while wide awake. This all sounds pretty crazy, right? I used to think I was crazy too. Once I used my wits to delve deeper into the nature of intuition, however, I discovered that there is nothing crazy about it.

Intuition is the ability to perceive information from a source other than the five physical senses. It's an ability commonly associated with the feminine. In a male-dominated society, women's intuition suffers by association. Women are more attuned to intuition than our male counterparts, genetically hardwired to access psychic communiques. Intuition is considered the female means of understanding the world, and reasoning the male—and superior—way. Women's intuitive ability is disparaged, minimized, and feared by those who don't want to acknowledge it.

In truth, reason and intuition are both necessary tools for understanding existence. It's time to correct the pervasive imbalance in vogue at the moment. As you will see, establishing this balance is not only a necessary step for female empowerment, it's critical for human survival. We, as women, bring life into this world. It's up to us to protect it.

Lorri Ann Devlin

# From Fearful to Fierce

THE NEGATIVE CULTURAL perception of intuition as the false notion of a simple mind discourages women from accessing, honing, and embracing our innate knowing. Habitual suppression of a useful survival tool isn't an ideal way to live our lives—it's the social equivalent of foot binding. It hobbles our stride and keeps us weak. I focus on women's intuition, but this book is beneficial to anyone who fears expressing his or her intuitive knowing, regardless of gender.

If you've had intuitive experiences, you may not talk about them outside a close circle of friends. While we no longer need to worry about finding ourselves bound to a post atop a blazing pyre, you may rightly worry about being subjected to a personal and professional barbeque. I certainly did.

This is a guide to understanding and reclaiming your hidden power, so it may guide your life. It's also the story of my personal transformation from a reluctant medium to one who wholeheartedly embraced her gifts. I hope you learn from my mistakes and successes. When I made the effort to examine my psychic experiences, I uncovered life-altering realizations about reality, time, and the afterlife. I didn't see any of that coming when I set out to explore an ability I didn't understand.

I've changed fear, anxiety, and self-doubt into profound gratitude. My gift brings me wisdom and serenity, and I want to show you how to have a richer life too. My story is both an instructional guide and a cautionary tale about the pitfalls of ignoring intuition.

When you exist in harmony with intuition, new excitement enters your life as you contribute to a higher purpose. As you'll learn, living an intuition-guided life improves the likelihood of our survival as a species. How's that for a win-win?

I promise it's possible to quiet skepticism and fear, maintain credibility, and use intuition to better your life. I did it. You will too.

Think about the shift that will happen as more of us reclaim the power of our inner knowing—a systematic erosion of negative societal judgment as we lead by example. The current mind-set about intuition forces us to ignore knowledge that is meant to provide a clearer understanding of ourselves and our world. It is a great tragedy to ignore such a valuable resource.

Once you master the art of intuition, you'll see that you've been struggling to catch the wind with a tear in your sails. Unless you mend that tear, you're not going to make consistent headway. It's exhilarating how much easier life gets when you're wide awake.

When you maintain a conscious connection to your rich database of intuitive knowledge, your path through life is clear. You're confident. You trust yourself, and you know who to trust. You enjoy a sense of unity with every living thing. You stop being scared. You catch a life-altering glimpse of eternity.

Embracing intuition taught me to see the world right in front of me in a new light. It will transform your life view as well. Your energy will shift. People will respond to you in a more respectful, attentive manner, without knowing why. You will command attention as you stride through life with a heightened sense of power and purpose. You will connect with others at a more satisfying level. Love will flow from you and into you. You will never be the same.

If you don't think you have intuitive abilities, read on. You'll be surprised to learn how perceptive you truly are. You haven't paid attention to the intuitive part of yourself because no one ever taught you how: I'm going to teach you. It'll be fun, I promise. You're going to discover you have a useful extra "brain" that you've never noticed.

## Reframing Intuition

It's not easy to embrace a talent that a culture doesn't accept as real. I'm asking you to trust that intuition is every bit as real and important as the information you obtain via reasoning and the five senses; trust that you're hardwired to use both reason and intuition to guide you. This book will allay your hesitation and enable you to embrace your gift.

## The Master Plan

My mission is to give intuition a much-needed cultural makeover. I began this task by conducting a preliminary research of the literature. Unable to find works that explored intuition's role in American culture, I broadened the search to texts about intuition in general. Very few resonated. Intelligent, accessible narratives that avoided excessive New-Age mysticism were in short supply. The pedantic philosophy texts I plowed through made me yearn for a decipherability app. It's been noted that brilliant minds often lack the ability to translate their ideas into language accessible to the layperson. What good is a brilliant idea if no one understands it?

Famed editor, writer, and philosopher Ruth Nanda Anshen, recognized this limitation of great minds: think of the old story of ten blind people each feeling a separate part of an elephant and then describing the creature solely based on their singular observation. She recognized that cross-specialty communication catalyzes progress and made it her mission to get diverse disciplines talking.

Anshen created connections between the great thinkers of different fields, offering them opportunities to explain their work to each other and to the general public. While studying for her PhD under the philosopher Alfred North Whitehead at Boston University in the late 1930s, Anshen was distressed to realize the extent to which the masters of various disciplines—such as physicist Albert Einstein and geneticist J.B.S. Haldane—seemed unaware of each other's work. She began editing the Science of Culture series in 1940, bringing together essays by luminaries as varied as Albert Einstein, Margaret Mead, Jonas Salk, and Thomas Mann in hopes of creating a unified theory to explain the workings of the universe through a cross-pollinating, multidisciplinary approach.

She also edited the Perspectives in Humanism, Religious Perspective, and World Perspective series, as well as a thirty-volume collection of intellectual autobiographies called Credo Perspectives, all with the intention of creating cross-disciplinary solutions to the world's problems. The World Perspective series included *The Art of Loving* by Erich Fromm and *Letters from the Field,* by Margaret Mead, both considered vital texts in their fields. Anshen wrote *The Mystery of Consciousness: A Prescription for Human Survival.* Her explanation of intuition as a survival strategy is seminal. She understood, as I do, that consciousness is a multifaceted state that embodies intuition. Consciousness enables human beings to interpret themselves and their relationship with the world around them. It is therefore an inseparable part of the workings of the mind. This is the crux of what I've come to understand about human intuition. It is inseparable from our very nature. Traditional science fragments the mind, cleaving intuition from reason, thereby obscuring this truth. The pervasive scientific fragmentation of the human mind splits professional disciplines and curtails rational discourse of intuitive knowing. In the space between Anshen's writing in the 1990s and the present day, scant philosophical progress is to be found.

Contemporary books about intuition are heavy on psychobabble and light on philosophy and science, which effectively limits broad acceptance. Since I couldn't find an intelligent mainstream discussion about intuition's place in our lives and culture, I set out to write one. I hope it appeals to your sensibilities as a person anxious to fill the emptiness you no doubt sense in our collective societal heart. The emptiness is real. It's the hole where intuition, the great unifier of humanity, is supposed to reside. Bad things are starting to happen because we're not thinking and reacting with full-brain capacity. An infection of disconnection has set in, and it's going to take a collective effort to restore intuitive health.

The good news is that advances in science, philosophy, and human evolution are not the sole responsibility of great thought leaders. Everyday people have the capacity to advance humanity by changing the way they think. It requires a subtle shift, that's all—a quiet intuition revolution.

When humanity allows inner knowing to be its guide, harmony is the result. Let's remove the shroud of fear and repression blanketing intuition and use our gift to repair this fragmented world.

## CHAPTER 1

# Embracing the Mystery

WHAT WOULD YOU think if I told you your intuitive life experiences are proof of a grand unified theory of existence, one that reveals a cosmic secret sought by humanity since we first arrived on mother Earth? Like Dorothy Gale, who believed she needed someone else (the Wizard of Oz) to tell her how to get home, we already possess the knowledge we need. Dorothy's dilemma is a metaphor for our condition as a species, disconnected from our inner knowing. We don't need the skills of a wizard or a PhD in quantum physics to find the way home. All that's required is an understanding of intuition. That's what I discovered when I stopped being scared to death of my psychic abilities and started applying deductive reasoning to the mix.

Science takes us partway on the existential journey, but the final leg ends right here, within ourselves. I've told you the end of the story. Now let's fill in the gaps leading up to this uplifting truth. Let's begin with the basics—Intuition 101: There is nothing extraordinary about extrasensory perception. Everyone has it, but like most aptitudes, it manifests in varying degrees. Everyone can hum, but we can't all sing like rock stars.

I have above-average psychic ability, probably to compensate for areas where I'm deficient, like mathematics and the capacity to understand why people get excited about sports and NASCAR. But even people who don't believe they have a lick of intuition are born with an intuitive connection to other living things.

I hid my abilities from others (and myself) out of fear of being called crazy. I ignored crucial information my brain was trying to share, much to my detriment. If I had paid attention to the not-so-quiet inner voice of intuition (sometimes it screamed, but I still didn't listen), I would not have chosen false friends and duplicitous business associates, eaten that bad shrimp, or done countless other embarrassing and unhelpful things.

Twenty-plus years of experience as a professional in healthcare research and business have taught me that the majority of my peers don't give a shred of credibility to intuition. They see demonstrations of psychic knowledge as nothing more than a clever parlor game. Most people want to believe that departed loved ones are a wavelength away and that the future is predictable, and skeptics consider psychics to be posers who use keen observational tricks to manipulate and appease the vulnerable.

Western culture views psychic ability as an amusing fantasy of the dimwitted. If you say you believe in intuition, Western science will smile at you with condescension, like you're a macaque attempting to impersonate a human. Next comes the inevitable parting shot: "But you can't *prove* it—not through the scientific method." Science is valuable. So is the study of intuition—it just requires a different lens. Who said there's just one way to perceive reality?

I've been intuitive since I was a little girl, before I knew what intuition was. I didn't know it was regarded differently than other abilities. I was psychic before I became a grown up, a nurse, or a parent. I didn't learn the truth of my talent through reductionist scientific method. I learned by permitting myself to experience intuition without judgment. That took some doing.

I'm a fan of reason. In an unrelenting quest for clarity, I pick at questions until they bleed. This drives my husband (and others, no doubt) to distraction. I require a high degree of intellectual orderliness. Not everyone cares to explain their statements in the meticulous logical detail I demand, which makes me annoying sometimes. As my husband put it, "I have to remember to think hard about what I'm about to say, because you're actually listening."

The problem is, intuition is inscrutable when stared down with reason. It must be examined in alternate ways to be understood.

My intuition takes the forms of premonitions, visions, and the sensation of an expanded boundary of self that doesn't stop at my physical periphery. I have spiritual visitations from people who are dead. All of this is discordant with reason until one grasps the truth that reason and intuition are different filters for perceiving reality. They're equally accurate. This truth required a shift in my reason-based thinking, an expansion of my perception of the nature of reality.

Psychic ability has enabled me to shift the way I perceive myself, from an isolated particle of humanity wandering the earth in a state of lonely existential angst to part of an interconnected whole. That's why I wrote this book: to share the process that led me to this happy conclusion, sparing you years of stumbling around trying to figure it out on your own.

Explanations of how great it is that we're all one, happy interconnected blob of consciousness aren't generally well received at social gatherings. That's the problem with our overly rational culture: it's not cool to be crazy like that. Because of its sketchy rap, people blessed with heightened intuition keep it hidden. Fearful of ridicule, we isolate and ignore this curious part of ourselves. We rarely talk about it, even amongst friends; therefore, we don't learn that intuitive experiences are in fact ubiquitous.

Intuition 101 isn't taught in elementary school, or Girl Scouts, or church. Babies learn the names of physical body parts from their parents. Kindergarten teachers introduce letters, numbers, manners, and the concepts of sharing and cooperation. We learn to read, write, use mathematics, and apply reason to solve problems. We are not taught that we possess a spiritual appendage called intuition. We don't know our third eye exists and therefore don't know how to open and use it. Sometimes it opens on its own, like it did for me. As a little girl, I assumed everyone else had a wide-open third eye.

Religious education is useful for opening the third eye because it teaches prayer, a meditative state conducive to intuitive flow. Prayer facilitates the expression of things unseen but deeply felt. However, church gets demerits, too, for being judgmental about psychic ability, often with terminal consequences.

Kids don't talk about intuitive experiences in the cafeteria. Not a single child uttered a word about intuitive knowing to me during my eight years as a school nurse. They didn't have a language to express it.

It's well documented that bullying and social isolation give rise to vulnerability in the forms of fear and anger. I saw this time and again as a school nurse working with traumatized children. Evolution has taught us to either hide or fight like hell when we find ourselves separated from the pack. We only feel safe when united. Outcast souls withdraw or lash out. There's a lot of this going on in our world as I write. Nationalism is a form of self-protective isolationism. It's what I call the infection of disconnection.

We notice this societal trend on the nightly news, and we sense it with our intuition. There is a global loss of cohesiveness, and it literally feels sad. The cause has little to do with issues of race or ethnicity, although prejudices surrounding our superficial external differences certainly play a part. It has to do with gender inequality, protective reflexive isolation, and spiritual hunger. Down deep where intuition lives, we don't feel safe because we're disconnected. We know there is power in unity, but we don't know how to achieve reunification. Instead, we retreat. We're going the wrong way, like a drunk driver hurtling up the wrong side of the freeway. We've lost vibrant, healing human connection. We've forgotten how to hear the sensible inner voice that dutifully warns of danger, urges us to sense our unity, and reminds us to love and protect one another.

*That inner voice is a survival message for our species.*

Call the voice what you choose, whatever your faith dictates. I call it the Consciousphere, the collective consciousness. Its language is intuition. Intuitive knowing is a nearly forgotten code for our survival. We're not going to hear it and heed it unless we start tuning in again.

Women must lead the charge, because we're superior communicators blessed with an abundance of intuitive power. Despite the fact we've been conditioned to ignore our gift by a society that says it doesn't exist, we're still able to hear the quiet voice of truth with practice. Your inner knowing is sacred. Don't let anyone take that truth away.

If you're a military veteran (my heartfelt thanks for your service, and God bless you), please understand that I'm not suggesting intuition alone can save our species. We need warriors to fight battles. If you're a scientist, thank you for your valuable contributions. But I'm begging you not to deny that every great discovery begins with a spark of intuition. And let's be honest, science really doesn't have any idea whatsoever where we came from, or where we're going. Intuition does.

So how do we resurrect intuitive power to its rightful place?

It will be a subtle revolution because celebrity psychic personalities aside, most intuitive people are quiet, sensitive souls. We're noticers—reflective, contemplative folks. We're hardwired to experience the world on multiple wavelengths. Many are artists, photographers, writers, and poets. We're nurses and teachers, lovers not fighters. We're the people with whom others feel comfortable confiding secrets because they sense our compassion. Fortunately, compassionate activists have wrought profound cultural changes in the past and can do so again.

We'll prevail by illuminating the planet with more and more awakened people who know how to focus heightened awareness. We will act and make decisions grounded in the truth that we are one unified being. Intuition will be restored to its powerful seat. The quiet power of interconnected minds shifting their perception of reality will effect change. Anyone who's part of a prayer circle can attest to this truth. You don't need to be affiliated with a religion or even believe in a higher power to accept that conscious intention is transformative. Our collective consciousness can and does create change in the world. What possible harm can ever come from living in conscious awareness of our interconnectedness? Only good comes from living this truth.

Don't worry if you fear you don't possess intuition. I bet you're able to sense nurturing compassion in fellow human beings. That's a form of knowing. Certain people feel good to be around. You gravitate to them. Others give you the creeps, even if you can't explain why. You instinctively respond to unconscious knowing. Take heart. Your instinct knows how to tap your intuition.

# CHAPTER 2

## Coming Out of the Cosmic Closet

IT'S NOT EASY to talk publicly about intuition and keep your credibility. It's harder still if you're an anxiously introverted person like me. I inherited an awkward social-anxiety gene from dear old dad. I imagine it huddled off in a corner, separated from the rest of the DNA strand, biting its nails. This anxious gene causes me to scrutinize my social performance during and after events involving people. I'm a self-conscious public speaker. I learned early on that speaking up was dangerous. I was ridiculed for holding beliefs or stating opinions contrary to my family's code of accepted behavior. I might get a slap across the face, a belt across my backside, or a bar of soap jammed in my mouth—not a recipe for cultivating a confident, outgoing young person.

My childhood was spent trying and failing to meet unrealistic standards of behavior. It was easy to step out of line, so I tried to be seen and not heard. These days, if I'm in a small group of trusted friends, and maybe there's wine, I'm a psychic chatterbox. I'll share that your grandmother—the one who left you her oval cameo brooch when she passed, and who skinny-dipped with your grandfather after her high-school graduation—is here and wants to say hello. But this merlot-enhanced openness about my ability took years to cultivate.

In my family, drawing attention to oneself was bad. Notice me, and I'd fret myself into a constellation of flaws. I didn't dare talk openly about my psychic ability. I barely had normal social ability. I'm an introvert by nature, and I don't enjoy the spotlight. I'm not seeking psychic celebrity. That's not my motivation for writing this book. My coming-out party is all about you, not me. I'm sharing my story to help you write your own. I find the media's treatment of psychic abilities troubling—it perpetuates the depiction of individuals with extrasensory perception as freaks. I get that it's entertaining to watch psychics pull facts out of thin air, but I'll be more content when intuition is acknowledged to be sacred and mundane.

Why do women hesitate to discuss intuition in their private lives? First, some may not be aware they possess it. It's hidden, sort of like a vagina. As a kid, if no one told you it's there, how would you know? Most psychic women I interviewed for this book admitted that they don't freely disclose their intuitive ability or experiences out of fear of being called crazy. There's too much risk of harsh judgment. As kids, we don't know that innate intuitive ability isn't okay to express. When we're little, we carry our true, happily interconnected nature around with us everywhere, like Linus and his blanket.

In early childhood we're feral, undomesticated creatures who utterly accept our true nature. We're fine with running around naked and a host of other socially frowned upon activities like biting, eating with our fingers, and not using toilets. When I was a kid, I assumed that *everyone* could see and talk to people who didn't happen to still be wearing their bodies. It was just a thing I did, like skipping, watching *Lost in Space*, and playing kick the can.

I was a happily intuitive kid. I found lots of four-leaved clovers; I just sensed where they were. I found coins the same way, instinctively using my sixth sense. It felt like a gravitational pull toward a picture I held in my mind. I followed the picture and the pull until I found what I was looking for. I got a validating rush of elation each time I followed the pull and found the treasure.

I literally shook the first hundred or so times I said out loud, "I have intuition." There are few respectable societal role models for us to emulate. I'm not aware of a single widely known disclosure by a respected world figure—or even a scene from a musical.

When I was thirty, I founded my first business. I was president and CEO of a national pharmaceutical and biotech consulting firm. I was lucky to have a skill set that was in high demand as insurance companies made sweeping changes to health-care delivery. Drug companies were competing to position their products on HMO and PPO formularies, and I was able to leverage the expertise in health insurance-managed care I acquired from my days with John Hancock Financial Services—they paid me well to champion their cause with payers. My company also developed and managed patient assistance programs for people who couldn't afford the exorbitant cost of prescription medication.

The big salary was nice, but I fought pretty much every breathing moment for credibility in a sexist, male-dominated industry. Men shrivel at the sight of a female CEO. They have no idea how to relate to a woman at the top of the food chain. Unable to process power and pantyhose comingling on the same body, my male coworkers regressed to their Neanderthal roots and tried to smite me as a threat to their dominance—that or seduce me. Sometimes they did both. It was stressful slogging through all that testosterone. Intuition subconsciously fueled my entrepreneurship, but admitting to psychic ability would've crushed my reputation. I hid my intuition so well that I couldn't find it when I needed its wisdom. I've neglected my intuition so badly that I'm surprised it still speaks to me.

You might be doing the same thing right now, anxiously stifling your inner voice and getting all confused in life as a result. You don't have to trade your hard-won credibility for the right to own your intuition. You get to have both. The first step is to acknowledge your intuition as an intelligent, creative, kickass part of yourself rather than as proof you're destined for a creaky institutional bed with wrist restraints. Your inner voice is real. Own it. The universe is literally calling you. If you'd like our species to evolve into something you wouldn't be ashamed to bring home to your parents, it's time to roll up your psychic sleeves like Rosie the Riveter and flex that intuitive muscle.

The first, biggest step before going public is to understand and accept your gift. Here's how I did it.

# CHAPTER 3

# Pagan Ghost Whisperer

FOR DECADES, I had a fearful fascination—an inner approach-avoidance dance—with my abilities. Why did I have premonitions? What caused them? What was their purpose? *Was there a purpose?* How could I see and feel people who had died? Like most people, I'm uncomfortable with things I can't control. I spent hours attempting to understand the logic of my experiences.

A little history: I was the first child born into my grandfather's household. Grampa Pete was a gentle giant of a man—a happy, blue-eyed Irishman and beloved chief of police in our suburban Boston town. He and his wife Marianne had one child together, my father Jack. Jack survived a sickly childhood, graduated college with a degree in electrical engineering, and got married—all without leaving home. He wed my mother, Gyneth, the year following his mother's death. At twenty-two, my mother became the nervous new woman of the house. I arrived nine months later, and three more babies followed. My siblings and I were the fourth generation to call the old, white colonial with three bedrooms and a single bath home.

My parents didn't allow misbehavior and disobedience. Ever. This included normal sibling rivalry, the kind that helps kids learn to resolve conflicts. I felt unrelenting pressure to be perfect before I realized this was impossible. By the time I reached school age, I'd internalized the message: I was a shameful, flawed child at risk of causing great shame and embarrassment to my family every time I opened my mouth. My grandfather's unconditional love salvaged me from a complete loss of self-esteem, but I wonder why he didn't step in more often when his grandchildren were under fire. I imagine he didn't want to overstep his bounds.

The result of my stern upbringing was a long personal struggle for basic self-acceptance. It was even longer before I allowed my submerged voice to surface.

## Nature's Role in Awakening Intuition

I was a sensitive kid who felt more at home in nature than anywhere else. I felt a connectedness in nature that superseded all other bonds. Nature was my first love, and I defended her. Litter was the enemy, along with big corporations and strip mining.

After pesticide trucks made their insidious crawl through the neighborhood spraying toxic clouds of DDT, I ran outside to rescue robins as they dropped moribund from the trees. I never saved one, but Lord, I tried. I felt a deep responsibility for my fellow creatures. But more than that, I experienced their sickness. Waves of nausea and dizziness passed through me as I tended my dying patients. I felt their distress in my body.

At around that time, I discovered Rachel Carson, the prophetic environmentalist and author of *Silent Spring*. She became my heroine. She represented the good that comes from living in harmony with the natural world. Her work is a passionate testament to our interconnectedness with nature. I had a pagan's wild heart, and Rachel Carson spoke to the intuitive truth I already knew. We are not outside of nature. We are of it.

I didn't have many close friends, choosing instead the quiet comfort of nature as my companion. I was an unusual, somewhat sad child, but my connection to nature was rejuvenating. It offered the experience of unconditional love, something lacking in my human relationships.

Grampa Pete and I shared a reverence for the earth and its beauty. From as far back as my memory goes, I loved working beside him in the garden. While immersed in fragrant loam and blooming flowers, I enjoyed a sense of well-being and connectedness. The back field was a natural playground where grass grew taller than my head. At night, the field was the perfect spot for firefly hunting. During the day, we chased butterflies with homemade nets fashioned from old broom handles, bent-wire coat hangers, and cheesecloth. I remember staring at grasshoppers for hours, watching the way their jaws moved sideways as they ate and marveling at their enormous eyes. Ladybugs, praying mantises, and caterpillars went about their lives alongside me, their giant admirer.

I felt the trees, flowers, and grass as living beings. As you can imagine, this made me an odd, dreamy sort of child. I made adults nervous. I wish I'd been a more outgoing and confident kid, but then I wouldn't have had the intense experience of nature that sustained me.

Communion with nature nurtured my ability to hear my inner voice. I followed it to a place of healing. As a child, I understood that nature is a realm without expectations, a world where I could not fail.

I gave myself up to its wild grace, and it soothed my soul. I felt calm in nature. I was free of the chronic tension that infused me and my household most of the time. During my darkest days, nature saved my life. I'll still take a forest over a function any day.

I feel most alive in the company of wild things. Red-tailed hawks seem to like me. I don't know why. Most days, no matter where I am, I see a red-tailed hawk. When I worked in Boston, a red-tail hawk used to perch on the ledge outside my window.

Getting out in nature is a powerful way to get in touch with your intuitive knowing. If you live in the city, find a place where something is growing. Sit on a bench and notice how many living things are nearby. Feel rain fall on your face. Breathe in the night. Smell the earth. Plant a small garden, or buy a single, fragrant potted basil plant. Inhale. Listen to birdsongs. There's a world of life around you. Feel your place as just one sentient life in a web of sentient beings, not at its center as self-awareness leads us to assume. Study the rough bark of a tree, or the pattern of netted veins, so like our own, on a leaf. You may not feel different right away. This is just practice connecting to a larger self.

Nature's rich symbolism is present in intuitive experience. One of the most healing visions I experienced, in fact, took the form of a great bird. I have anxiety about air travel, and the night before my flight to a brain research conference, I had a vivid dream. I flailed in a tossing sea, and an enormous bird swooped down to rescue me. I felt secure and safe wrapped in the protective layers of her immense, impenetrable white feathers, strong as chain mail. Her wings were a fortress. I sank into her embrace and felt peace.

The morning of the flight was stormy. Later, as the plane pitched and rolled in heavy turbulence, the bird reentered my thoughts. As the plane shuddered and shook, I held an image of myself, the passengers, and the entire plane wrapped in the steady, strong wings of the great white creature. It was like someone had said "You're safe" aloud—in that instant, the plane stopped shaking and leveled. The loud rumbling stopped, and a smooth landing ensued.

In times of great stress, when I've faced surgery or a loved one's imminent departure, the vision of the luminous creature who cradled me in her wings returns.

Most adults are aware of their interconnectness only sporadically, through isolated events like my dream. Infants and children, on the other hand, experience their connection consistently. Newborns come into the world with an innate, albeit unconscious, awareness of their interconnectedness with nature. Before physical birth, we are part of an undifferentiated whole. We long to return to that state, and we carry the ache of separation in our psyche. Living an intuitive life, including regular meditation in nature, is a lifeline back to the experience of oneness disrupted when we're born into a body.

Do you want to feel your connection to something larger? Ask. Invite the experience into your life. Then be still, as if you're in the forest waiting for a doe to venture into view. If you're more of an indoor person, appreciate the way light slants across your floors in the afternoon. Notice how light illuminates your living space. Look out the window at scuttling clouds. Watch the fog roll in with a cup of ginger tea. Observe flowers nodding in a gentle wind. Read poetry. Practice yoga or meditation. Listen to Mozart. There are many ways to connect with one's higher awareness. If your vehicle isn't nature, find what it is, and let it lead you.

## Ghosted

My path to connectedness with higher awareness was solitude. Since I did my best to keep a low profile in my childhood home, I spent a lot of time in isolated play. During my quiet, alone time I saw all kinds of fascinating things unfold. As early as age three, I was chatting with a little boy no one else could see. I didn't consider this unusual. Kids accept all kinds of things as normal until we teach them otherwise.

In a house that had been home to generations of ancestral inhabitants, several of whom had breathed their last in its rooms, it isn't surprising that a little girl with intuition would have a psychic field day. My best friend was a frail, friendly little boy with light brown hair and pale skin. We had hours of animated conversations, and he told the most wonderful stories. I wish I could recall what we talked about! He was captivating, with mischievous eyes and a sweet smile. One day my mom asked me who I was talking to. No one else was in the room. I assumed she could see my friend. I was three, and I'd never asked him his name—names weren't a big thing with me. But I had to answer, so I made up a name. "It's Tom."

Tom and I visited by the fireplace in the living room. He liked being close to the hearth. My mom humored me and set a place at the table for Tom at lunchtime. Looking back, I realize I wasn't seeing Tom with my eyes, although that didn't register until later. I saw him in another way. And while I recall us having long, wonderful conversations, we never used words.

Years later, I came upon a photograph of Grampa Pete's youngest brother, a frail boy who died in the devastating influenza epidemic of the early 1900s. He was five years old, and he had light brown hair, pale skin, and the mischievous eyes and sweet smile I knew so well. It was Tom! But his real name was Myles. I'm glad he didn't mind my mistake—I'm not good with names.

When I realized that my mother couldn't see Tom/Myles, I understood that I was different. This was unsettling. I continued to have psychic experiences, but I didn't talk about them. I tried to figure out what was happening on my own. My dad placed a high value on intelligence and effective problem-solving, and I figured

I should be able to sort out the answers. That was safer. In my family, asking for help could prove dangerous. When I couldn't solve problems on my math homework, my frustrated dad's way of "helping" was to slap me on the back of the head and say, "Think, dammit!" Dad and I had many tender moments, and he could be a gentle, loving man, but he was a terrible math tutor.

So, for the next twenty years, I kept my mouth shut and surreptitiously studied psychic phenomenon with the devotion of a scientist. I was a very reluctant medium. Please, don't do what I did. Don't let fear keep you from embracing your gift. I took years (suffering, learning, failing, and learning from failing) to come to terms with my intuition. I speak from experience when I share this truth—when you conquer your fears of judgment and of being "out of control" and invite a connection, intuition flows. Your path reveals itself. You experience signs everywhere. Fear vanishes. Serendipity becomes commonplace. Love and creative energy flow. You flourish.

## CHAPTER 4

— ✧ —

# Learning to Work Your Own Mind

An intuition cannot be proven; it is experienced.

—Gaston Bachelard

Intuitive knowledge is larger than I am. It flows through me like a river through a hollow reed. Its power must be felt to be understood. If you've never thought yourself capable of intuitive insight, you may have doubts. Skepticism is fine, so long as it doesn't extinguish curiosity. Every scientist is a skeptic. But she's also a dreamer. This book is data. Dissect it. Add your ideas to my theory of intuitive knowing as proof that a loving consciousness unites us.

The Consciousphere is our spiritual atmosphere. It's indivisible. It does not begin and end within a human body, and it doesn't die when the body does. Intuition is the language of the universe, your personal gateway to the Consciousphere and glimpse into eternity. This is the startling yet logical conclusion I reached after years of being a reluctant medium. Psychic awareness proves we coexist on an eternal main server after our peripheral hardware fails. I have proof. One day, my motherboard crashed, and I nearly died. Instead of seeing the blue screen of death, I visited the next phase of life.

I'll explore this incident in detail later, but I have less dramatic psychic experiences every day. You do too, but you may not be paying attention (yet). Even with training, I miss occasional subtle messages. Others won't stop niggling me until I acknowledge them. Once, for example, I was in Bermuda on vacation with friends. We were out to dinner when suddenly (it's always suddenly), the spirit of an infant boy nudged me as I sipped a dark and stormy. The boy wanted me to tell his brother—the busy hipster bartender up to his man bun in drink orders—that he was present. I got the familiar rush of introverted angst. Mediumship often comes with compulsive urges to share something intimate and unusual with a complete stranger, often in a public forum.

I took a gulp of liquid courage to help me get up the nerve to ask the busy millennial bartender an outlandish question.

"Excuse me, this is a strange question, and we haven't met, but do you have a little brother?"

"No."

Whoa. That never happens. I hesitated. The baby wouldn't give up. He was still with me, waiting.

After a pause, the bartender spoke again, without ceasing his frenetic whir of movement behind the bar. "Well, yes. I mean, I did. But he died when he was a baby, ten months before I was born. I never knew him."

This guy registered no particular interest in my question. That was unusual. When a spirit visits, it's always because there's a willing receiver. That doesn't stop me from the familiar "eek, what if I'm wrong this time?" reluctance before I share a psychic message.

Then it hit me: the message wasn't meant for the busy bartender. The little boy was trying to reach someone else. When Man Bun returned to my end of the bar, I flagged him down.

"Will you give your mom a message? She needs to hear that her other son is with her." The little spirit bathed me in love as I shared this, a sure sign I'd gotten his message right.

The whirling bartender stood still and looked me straight in the eye. I (we) had his attention. "Oh, for sure. I definitely will. She's way into this stuff."

And off he went with a tray of mojitos.

I hoped he told his mom that her first son, for whom she still grieved, was with her, at peace, and loving her in the next phase of life.

Experiences such as this are what convince me that our separateness is illusory. It's clear we're connected in one big glob of consciousness. How else can I discern truths about total strangers and spirit beings? I ruled out the possibility that I was simply picking up people's memories or thoughts. That's true sometimes, but it feels different than when I'm in touch with conscious beings. They feel different than thought waves. Their presence is more palpable than a living human's. The only logical answer is that we're merged outside body and time. If you have a better theory, please e-mail me: I want to hear it.

As extraordinary as it is to suggest spirits are conscious living beings and time isn't linear, I'm far from the first rational person to do so. I'm late to this party; it's hard to avoid being derivative when writing about existence and consciousness. I studied metaphysical and scientific works by poets, philosophers, and scientists. James Hillman, Stephen Hawking, Lao Tse, Jonas Salk, Paul Davies, Sant Kirpal Singh, and Osho, are a few of my teachers.

## Mastering the Mind

When my son was six, I told him a story. When he was three years old, we'd attended his aunt and uncle's wedding, where his cousin had participated as the ring bearer. My son was angry that his dad and I hadn't invited him to be the ring bearer at our ceremony. I explained that he hadn't been born yet, so we'd had to give the job to someone else. After a pause, he said, "You know, Mom, when you're a kid, sometimes you don't know how to work your own mind."

It is a rare person who masters her own mind. When you find your internal GPS, it's a transformative first step. In his best-selling book *Biocentrism*, Robert Lanza turns reality inside out as he explores the role of the human mind in the creation of reality. He posits that human consciousness creates what we perceive as reality. In other words, reality doesn't exist outside of the mind: we bring it to life when we observe it. We construct it through our sensory faculties.

I contend that the Consciousphere permeates us—it does not originate within us. We filter consciousness through sensory faculties and the brain, creating a sensory-based image of the matrix of which we are part and parcel. The picture we perceive is partial, restricted by biological limitations. The Consciousphere looks different depending on who's doing the looking.

## Listening to the Radio

The drive to understand psychic ability led me down a philosopher's path and opened my eyes to a bigger reality. You can find your way to that bigger reality too. Let's start with an exercise that describes the process of receiving information from the Consciousphere:

Imagine you're on your couch, watching a good show. You're immersed in the drama, eating popcorn and listening to the dialogue between actors. As you watch, you become aware that out in the kitchen, there's a radio show playing.

The radio is tuned low, but if you shift your attention away from your popcorn and the movie, you can make out the announcer's words. You catch a phrase or two. If you mute your TV set, you improve your ability to hear the radio voice.

The radio broadcast is coming from the Consciousphere. It's not mind chatter, the self-talk where we think, "Oh, I have to remember to buy milk on the way home," or "I'll never make this deadline." It's easy to confuse the two. The radio broadcast is not you talking to yourself. It's the Consciousphere talking to you. At first it's difficult to distinguish between your self-talk and intuitive communication. Don't worry about that. With practice, you'll sense the subtle difference. I notice that my mind chatter is accompanied by mild anxiety since that's what is generating it. Intuitive broadcasts don't feel like they're coming from you, they feel like they're coming to you.

When I mute the volume of my TV, (my myriad thoughts and distractions), I comprehend the information on Consciousphere radio. I recognize that the radio's been on my whole life, but that I haven't been paying attention.

The broadcast may be something simple, as when it tells me, "Jean is going to call today." Later, Jean calls. That's when I remember the earlier predictive message I half ignored. The Consciousphere often speaks in daydreams. Daydreams are rich in intuitive guidance—pay attention to their content. It may be puzzling or seem like nonsense, but chances are high those dreams are telling you something important.

Let's return to my Bermuda holiday for an example. My friend Peter was stung by a bee while at the beach. As I dashed up the steps from the shore to our cottage for ice and Benadryl (he has a history of allergic response to bee stings), I recalled that moments earlier, I'd been daydreaming of bee stings, apropos of nothing. It was October, and we were on a beach in Bermuda. I hadn't seen a bee, nor am I an apiphobe who obsessively ruminates on the topic. My daydream was a precognitive warning. Even with heightened awareness, however, I occasionally ignore a predictive message. I catch more now that I've trained myself.

Had I been better attuned to my intuitive premonition, I would have said "Hey, Peter, I remember you're allergic to bees. Did you bring your EpiPen with you?" This is a rational question, preferable to blurting, "I just had a morbid premonition of stinging bees—run away!" You can say just about anything to another person, depending on *how* you say it. This is important to remember when discussing your premonitions and sensitive intuitive intel with others.

Here's a meditative exercise to try when you're ready to quiet mind chatter and tune in to your psychic radio. I didn't invent it, but I've used it successfully:

Imagine you have the power to breathe under water through imaginary gills.

Next, place yourself comfortably at the bottom of a warm body of water. Far above you, a storm whips the water's surface. You know the storm is up there. But you are deep below, where the water remains quiet and still. You are not touched by the turbulence at the surface. You are surrounded by peace. Be aware of the storm. Let it be. Be aware of your detachment from the storm. Be aware of the stillness. Listen.

You are not listening for sounds. You are listening for stillness. Later, sounds will come. Like the radio in the kitchen, the sounds emanate from somewhere else. Some people see pictures instead of a voice or feel an intense emotion. A knowing. Everyone's experience is unique.

If you don't enjoy the idea of being under water, place yourself in another setting that feels peaceful. Create a safe space between you and a distant commotion that symbolizes mind chatter. Then ignore the commotion, and listen to the vast quiet beneath it.

The Indian mystic Osho recommends, "Listen to your being. It is continuously giving you hints; it is a still, small voice. It does not shout at you…And if you are a little silent, you will start feeling your way."

Don't be discouraged if it takes several attempts to find your way to inner knowing. It's more likely to come upon you sideways. Start out by practicing being a little silent, as Osho suggests. Intuition's natural habitat is the periphery. You're more likely to experience its flicker by focusing your gaze away and off to the side, the way you use your eyes in the dark.

There's great reward in tuning in to intuitive premonitions. When I attend to a message I've intuited, and it comes to fruition, I get a rush of elation. There's an exuberant "yes" moment that hits me in a surge of endorphins. I feel the truth of the experience in a rush of vibrant wellbeing.

By the way, the Benadryl worked, and Peter recovered from his bee sting with the help of topical ice and a tropical beverage.

Psychic knowing can also hit like a bolt of lightning rather than a quiet broadcast. I've been blasted by blaring air horn alerts that demand my undivided attention—"Red alert! Red alert! Deer about to jump in your path on the highway!" I slowed the car. The deer appeared where my car would have been if I hadn't heeded the warning. The deer bounded into the woods. I did yoga breathing to slow the palpitations. Whew. Thanks, intuition.

My friend Peter (the beesting survivor) reports that he has impending deer-in-the-headlights premonitions as well. It's a handy talent.

When an intuitive pop happens, I'm instantly aware of information without the help of traditional sensory delivery channels. Intuitive knowing skips the sensory ports that feed data to the brain. I have an immediate flash of knowing that bursts into awareness stronger than any traditional sensory message. It's a startling sensation that always surprises me. If you've ever been in a dark room and someone unexpectedly flips on a bright light, you jump. It's like that. It takes a moment to adjust to the new environment.

Premonitions come in all sizes. Sometimes they're warnings portending life-changing events; sometimes it's all about sandwiches. Recently my husband Steve told me he'd invited our college buddy Sam and his wife, Annie, whom we hadn't yet met, to our home for lunch. A fact lit up in my brain. "Annie can't eat gluten," I said aloud, without processing how I came to know this about a person I'd never met.

"How do you know?" Steve asked.

I didn't know how I knew. I'd just blurted out the data as it landed in my brain.

When our guests arrived, Annie thanked us for the invite, and as we sat down to lunch, she told me about her gluten sensitivity. I smiled. It's just so cool when this happens! I never get over the rush. It reminds me all over again how little we understand about this fascinatingly complex world of ours.

Annie was pleasantly surprised to find I had prepared her a gluten-free lobster roll, compliments of the inexplicable talent my kids used to call Mom's hippie magic. I've learned to be careful how, when, where, and what I blurt. I urge you to do the same, especially when you're new to disclosing your talent. Of course we should never share potentially frightening psychic material. I've seen psychics—and, often, imposters—do that, and it ticks me off. One such fool told my sister-in-law that her son had a demon attached to him. My sensitive sister-in-law was distraught by this tactless fraud's ridiculous claim.

I don't believe demons exist. And even if you do, it's not okay to scare nervous mothers out of their wits. Being psychic doesn't automatically make a person tactful or intelligent. I respectfully consider my audience and calibrate my delivery. I have a responsibility here. If I sense that a person with cancer is not free of disease, I don't say that. I say I'm sending healing energy. I affirm his or her diligent medical follow-up and healing-modality choices. I offer a reminder that hope is a strong drug.

I feel momentarily off balance whenever I blurt a harmless intuitive truth I have no logical way of knowing, like a gluten issue. This month I joined a garden club. I was a little nervous as the new person in a roomful of strangers. I was introduced to a slender woman in her seventies, and what was the first thing I said? "How long have you been living on a sailboat? I've always wanted to be a live-aboard!" I got the familiar quizzical stare and the "How did you *know* that?"

It's good to have a prepared statement for such occasions. I adopt a casual, matter-of-fact persona that hides the awkwardness of accidentally outing my hippie magic and say, "Oh, I have intuition. It runs in the family."

Downplaying my talent is a clever way to paint a message of normality and acceptance. My casual tone conveys the fact that really intuition is quite pedestrian. It's just proof we're one glorious, unified orb of consciousness, that's all. Neutral sharing moves us closer to a world where women's intuition is accepted and honored as a ubiquitous natural resource.

I wish I could come out and say "It's quite simple, once you discard the false pretense science holds about the nature of reality—you know, the one wherein there exists an irreconcilable dichotomy between the observer and the observed. Surely you glean how prescient thought and experience (not to mention the curious tendency of quantum particles/waves to react differently depending upon whether they're observed) proves our separateness is illusory?"

But I can't. Not if I want to get invited to parties once in a while. It's best to keep it simple. I suggest we continue to plant normalizing comments about our aptitude into everyday conversation, where seeds of acceptance will germinate and spread in the collective unconscious.

## Why I Don't Win Powerball

Some people use the inconsistent nature of intuition to negate its reality. That's the same as stating rain doesn't exist because sometimes it's sunny. Intuition is fickle. Why does it show me certain things and not others? Why am I always losing a half-full mug of coffee or a set of keys? Where's my intuition then? On a more consequential scale, why didn't I know that my youngest son was lonely for more attention from me when he was a young child? He was (and is) one of the greatest joys in my life. But I didn't sense the depth of his need, and I let him down. To his credit and my great relief, he forgave me. I'm still working on forgiving myself.

Why can't intuitive people pick winning lottery numbers? I did, once. My husband woke me from a dream, where I was seeing a string of lottery numbers. The four I remembered before he woke me came in, but I missed out on the big win.

I don't know why intuition is selective. There are elements of the gift I'll never understand, and that's okay. We can revel in the mystery. But not before dissecting it a bit more.

One reason we perceive intuition as selective may be a function of our limited capacity to attend. There are billions of bits of information hovering in the Consciousphere. Our minds can't attend to all that and focus on our day-to-day lives. If the theory of intelligent design, including predetermined cosmic destiny, is accurate, we're not meant to know the entire script, just what's required for our role.

There's a way to go after information in the Consciousphere rather than waiting for it to find us. This was a big revelation. When I focus on someone or something with intention, information that's relevant to my thoughts zooms into focus. Imagine it this way:

You're staring at a mist comprised of billions of tiny multi-colored particles hovering in space. You focus your thoughts on the color green. Since you're thinking green, that color leaps into sharper focus within the mist. As you tune into the green particles, the nongreen particles in the mist can be ignored. I've learned to seek out psychic intel using this technique. If someone asks me for information about a friend named John, I look into the mist and ignore all the not-John bits, until I find John.

# The C-Word: Enemy of the People

I interviewed many courageous intuitive women for this book. You'll read their fascinating accounts later. The women who came forward are articulate, and many are extraordinarily confident, accomplished people. Yet every single one prefaced her story with a variation of the same discrediting statement:

"You'll probably think I'm crazy…"

"This may sound crazy…"

"I know it's crazy…"

We've learned to preemptively discredit ourselves to save face. I don't believe any of the women who shared their psychic experiences truly believe they're crazy. They're conditioned to talk that way by a culture of disbelief.

Even when talking with me, a psychic author championing the truth of psychic awareness, they still used the c-word.

Please stop using the c-word when you dare to share your intuitive experiences. Own your power. This is your mandatory intuitive activist assignment.

# CHAPTER 5

—⚭—

# Prove It: Quieting the Skeptics

Intelligence is dangerous. Intelligence
means you will start thinking on your own;
you will start looking around on your own.
You will not believe in the scriptures; you
will believe only in your own experience.

—Osho

EVIDENCE-BASED RESEARCH IS the gold standard of scientific progress. It's a practice I became very familiar with as a clinical research manager in human trials for new drugs designed to combat the devastating effects of Alzheimer's disease. Some of the subjects—husbands, wives, and grandparents—would receive a placebo. Others would receive the new drug, which might or might not help—and could potentially harm. My duties included obtaining informed consent from study subjects and their family members, performing routine physical examinations, and meticulously documenting study data.

It was scientist nirvana. Reason ruled my careful study documentation, but intuition quietly guided my interactions with patients and families. Knowing how to read people's inner emotional states and relate accordingly was a tremendous asset as I guided families through a stressful process. I just couldn't talk about that easily with my peers. I respected my ability to be rational and analytical. Growing up in a chaotic environment cultivated a craving for order and predictability in me. I sought out positions that enabled me to work in organized, efficient environments. I began my nursing career at a world-renowned trauma center in Boston. I worked alongside researchers trying to improve treatment outcomes for people paralyzed by a spinal cord injury. In later years, I worked as a managed-care executive, where one of my responsibilities was to provide data to actuaries so they could demonstrate evidence to show that optimal health-care delivery results in cost savings.

But what constitutes evidence when we discuss the metaphysical world? Where is the evidence-based research for intuition? My proof is my personal experience. Metaphysical evidence is empirical. It is information acquired by observation and personal experience. My evidence is my life.

In the language of science, psychic ability is nonfalsifiable—it cannot be proved or disproved through traditional scientific research methods. But it does not follow that because something is nonfalsifiable, it doesn't exist. You can't prove feelings, either: desire, love, grief—all are nonfalsifiable, and all very real. We can watch a human brain light up on a PET scan as its owner experiences emotions, but the images are evidence of a feeling, not the feeling itself. We can't prove a thought. Try to prove the nature of music to a person who is deaf. Sounds waves exist, and mathematical rhythms can be transcribed and reproduced. But without functional hearing and a brain to translate sound waves, what is music? Can a person disconnected from their intuition refute it, even though others can sense theirs? Defining what's real isn't as easy as it seems.

Plato said, "Thou has seen the kettles of consciousness aboiling: consider also the fire." The brain is the kettle of Consciousphere aboiling; the Consciousphere is the fire. The "you" who stands apart and observes your own brain thinking is the blazing fire. Intuition is the spark that startles you into awareness.

If you're a scientist or an engineer by trade, or someone who's uncomfortable with things you can't measure, hang in there. I got dragged to this party, too, by possessing nonfalsifiable abilities. Don't prevent the inability to prove intuition using reason alone stand in the way of progress. Just because we can't prove we're all channeling a vast database doesn't mean that we won't be able to. An electroencephalogram reads invisible brain waves. Electrocardiograms convert the heart's electrical activity into visible patterns. Who knows what's possible down the road?

For now, personal and anecdotal experience is our proof. It is enough.

Going forward, our fearless sharing of intuitive experience will inspire debate and discovery. With that in mind, here's a ghost story.

# CHAPTER 6

# Living with Spirits

PRIVACY WAS RARE in a house with six rooms and seven people. I shared the master bedroom with three sisters. Before we were born, the bedroom had been my parents'—and my grandparents' before them. My dad was born in the room, and his mother had died in it, as had her father.

Our home and various outbuildings contained the possessions of generations. I liked to play there, surrounded by history. Ox bows, antique garden scythes, deer antlers, dusty wicker furniture, and old encyclopedias were fascinating keys to what had happened before I arrived on the scene. They helped me feel my place in the family lineage. Up in the attic, I found ornately illustrated history books, fancy hat boxes, intricately beaded gowns from galas past, and box upon box of photographs. Faces from the past smiled from decks of ocean liners. Jaunty men in motorcars tipped their scollay caps. Little children in knickers posed with scruffy dogs in the same yard where I played.

The attic was accessed through an upstairs linen closet. Inside the closet, there was a built-in chest of drawers. Above it, a trap door was cut into the ceiling. I had to pull out the drawers of the chest and use them as steps to reach the trap door. Once at the top of the chest, I stretched my arms up to slide the door open. A three-step wooden ladder nailed to the back wall served as the final steps up.

As I pushed my body through the opening, I entered a private enclave. The air stood still, an oasis of peace in a noisy household. The sweet smell of dry wood greeted me as I entered the company of gentle spirits.

I felt Grandma Marianne's presence as I held my dad's childhood books and board games and admired her silk dresses. As I looked through the old photos, I admired her stylish Roaring Twenties couture. A tender feeling enveloped me. She was letting me know her. I wasn't imagining her. I felt her actual presence.

She told me how much fun she'd had on the transatlantic cruise where she'd fallen in love with Grampa Pete. She told me she wished she'd lived to know me and my siblings in this life. She still watched over my dad, her only son, and she knew he was a difficult person to be around. He was smart, with a quick wit, but he didn't know how to relate to children. She shared these things without words, in the language of intuition.

I loved visiting with Grandma Marianne. The peace she gave me lingered long after I climbed out of the linen closet to join the family for supper.

Our piano used to play when no one was seated at the keys. The first time I heard it, I was upstairs in my bedroom. I thought Dad had come home early from work, since he was the only one who played so well. But he wasn't home, and no one was sitting at the piano when I went downstairs to check. The only other person who had played the piano was Grandma Marianne.

Visitations by dead relatives and mysterious piano music sound spooky, but I never felt afraid; I felt loved. It was just the way things were at my house. I accepted all sorts of things as normal before I was taught otherwise.

## CHAPTER 7

— ⁊ —

# Empathic Intuition

HAVE YOU EVER felt exhausted after being with certain people? They may seem pleasant enough, yet you feel depleted in their presence. When out in a public place, like a mall or restaurant, have you felt a wave of inexplicable sadness, excitement, anger, or fear? Have you found yourself in a disturbing daydream and thought, "Why am I thinking about this? It doesn't feel like me."

Maybe it's *not* you.

Empathic intuition is the ability to experience another's feelings and sometimes their accompanying thoughts as well. It's different from empathy, which is the ability to imagine and relate to the feelings of another. When I experience empathic intuition, it always unsettles me until I figure out that I'm feeling an emotion or channeling a thought that didn't originate within me. The idea seems preposterous, but it's true.

Empathic emotions and thoughts hit me with intensity. The downside of being connected to everyone and everything is that some unenlightened souls are angry. When I pick up thoughts from other drivers on the road, for example, it's easy to distinguish their hostile emotions from my own, since I love to drive and don't experience road rage. I'm happy to let speeding fools pass me. I'm a BMW performance aficionado, but I'm no daredevil. I'm often confronted by drivers who want to show me how fast their cars can go. It bothers them that I don't engage in road games. I let their negative emotions pass me in the high-speed lane. No need to hang on to those.

When I was little, I was often confused by emotions I didn't understand. They were bewildering things, well beyond the scope of my limited life experience. I felt oddly ancient, burdened by the weight of heavy feelings inside my small self. I had no idea that I was empathically experiencing the feelings of those around me. This ability is known as clairsentience. People who have clairsentience are known as empaths, although I don't like the term. It implies that's all I am. I'm not an empath. I'm a person with empathic ability. Being an empath means one literally feels the pain of another person or creature, as I did with those poor poisoned robins.

As a child, I felt a deep mantle of grief weighing me down before I ever experienced loss. Now I understand. Adults in my family were grieving silently all around me. I was born less than two years after my dad lost his mother, my grandma Marianne. He grieved her, and so did Grampa Pete. I was living in a house heavy with the unspoken grief of two stoic men. Like most men of their generations, they never spoke a word about their loss. I wish they had. It would have been easier to connect my grief feelings to an actual event.

I didn't grieve Grandma Marianne's loss because I felt her as a tangible presence everywhere in our home. She smiled when I sat in the living room and ran my fingers admiringly along the carved wooden arms of her Eastlake furniture. She stood behind me, an approving hand on my shoulder as I peered through the glass doors of her china cabinet, admiring the exquisite crystal stemware that no one in our family used anymore. She loved fine things, and she noticed my kindred appreciation.

It makes sense that I was able to feel the emotions of spirits as well as living human beings. Children are naturally empathic. Like most children, I had a sharp radar when it came to sensing my parents' feelings. Highly attuned empathic kids are either born exceptionally sensitive, or have honed the ability out of necessity, as in cases of trauma. The ability to sense impending trouble is a necessary survival skill in a volatile household. Best to know who's on the verge of exploding and seek cover.

My mother was an anxious woman who suffered unpredictable, extreme mood swings. As a child I sensed her distress and anxiety as my own. Of course, I had my own feelings about being helplessly reliant on an emotionally fragile mother, but there was more to it than that. I recall a day when I was four and she was uncomfortably pregnant, resting on the couch. I grabbed my belly as bands of pain radiated from her, mingled with tendrils of fear, and landed in me. I felt her pain. She cried when I took her hand and said, "Mommy, I wish I could take your pain away and put it inside me." The thing is, her pain was already inside me.

I felt happy energy too, so it wasn't all doom and gloom. My mom's friend Ramona brought a bouncy orb of dancing energy into the house when she visited. She crackled with creative sparks. Ramona's energy spilled into me like fizzy water, but I didn't have language to describe what I was feeling. Who does? We are not taught the language of intuition. Our culture denies it, so the experiences remain unspoken.

It's not easy being a human sponge. It can be confusing and exhausting. It took time for me to sort out when I was feeling an emotion or thought that didn't originate in my body. Eventually I learned. Now I put an imaginary but effective protective bubble around myself to keep those feelings from overwhelming me.

If you want to hone empathic abilities, start by noticing how you feel around certain people. When grumpy complainers make you inwardly roll your eyes and rude people generate feelings of annoyance, try listening to what's under your reflexive surface emotions to discern what your gut is feeling.

Do you have an uneasy sensation? Do you feel depleted or exhausted by the person? Don't try to analyze what you're feeling. It's usually entirely out of context with what your rational mind is processing about the person. Just note your impressions.

I feel empathic energy in my solar plexus, the area known in energy terms as the third chakra. You may feel empathic sensations in a different area of your body. Pay attention to what you feel and where you feel it. Start an intuitive journal and track your experiences.

If possible without causing harm or discomfort to yourself and the person you're reading, seek corroboration. You may not be able to if you're in a public place and pick up vibes from a stranger. This happens to me in restaurants. I'll say to my husband, "See that woman over there? She's furious and sad. Her husband is cheating on her, and she just found out. She's going to leave him." I don't walk over to her and ask for corroboration, I don't need validation anymore because I trust my knowing. But since you're starting out, affirmation is useful. Ask a friend who's open to helping, or a willing professional psychic.

As you practice empathic awareness, balance what you feel with what you know. Don't throw reason out the window. There's a difference between empathic knowledge and preconceived notions. If past experience with a person or group is fueling a perception, that's not empathic intuition. Your impression is more likely to be intuition if you can't logically trace its origin.

## CHAPTER 8

*∞*

# What's it Like Being a Medium?

I GREW UP empathic and aware of spirits, and my abilities strength-
ened as my brain developed. During childhood, the only ghost I
ever saw with my own eyes was my talking plush toy, Casper the
friendly ghost. I loved his cartoon TV series back in the sixties.
I was twelve before I encountered a real-life ghost. Here's what
happened.

My parents had bought a parcel of land on Cape Cod near
the banks of the Pocasset River, a salt-water stream that wound its
way inland from the upper east shores of Buzzards Bay. Buzzards
Bay is a windswept, shallow body of water between the Nantucket
and Rhode Island Sounds.

It was a short barefoot run from the end of the lane and a sandy embankment to the river where a world of nature awaited. To
the west, the surface waters of Buzzards Bay glittered with sunny
"Cape Cod diamonds." To the east, the river's source broadened
to form an estuary teeming with minnows, great blue herons,
egrets, gulls, and dozens of other bird species. It was paradise for
a nature-loving kid.

At the end of the day, we camped on our new land. We got along better in that tent than we did back at home. A kerosene lamp cast a happy glow over us. We sang songs, played word games in our sleeping bags, and fell asleep to the gentle hiss of the lamp and singing crickets.

The summer I turned twelve, my dad and Grampa Pete built a cottage on the land. They did most of the work themselves, aside from digging the foundation. For that, they hired a local man, Mr. Lindstrom. He was a tall, serious old man in baggy overalls covered with dust. Our cottage foundation was one of the last he completed before he died.

During the construction, I spent long hours playing at the river. My sisters weren't as outdoorsy as I was, so I was often happily alone. The river was mine. I had a deep sense of place there. I marveled at tiny sea creatures, sat in the cool sand under shady pines along the riverbank, and inhaled the fragrant sea breeze. With water lapping my feet and puffy clouds floating over my head, blissful oneness bathed my pagan soul.

I wasn't really by myself. I shared the river with spirits of the Wampanoag who had once fished its waters. They left behind arrowheads and other tools crafted from the abundant quartz and porphyry common to the region. Intuitive knowing linked us together, outside of time. We sensed one another, oblivious to the years that separated our human forms. I didn't see them, but I sensed them as if they were visible. I loved it when one of them led me to an arrowhead. I followed his or her beckoning until I found the treasure resting in wet sand at the low tide line or in the dry outwash at the riverbank's edge. When I held the arrowhead in my hand, it reverberated with the energy of the young man who made it. I have a collection of arrowheads I found by "feeling" my way to them. The spirits appreciated my admiration of their work and the fact that I bore witness to their continued existence. I knew I was among conscious beings. I never said to myself, "I'm a medium. That's why I can communicate with spirits." I didn't know the name for what I was, and I had no frame of reference for explaining it.

The cottage was mostly finished when I saw my first ghost. I was upstairs in bed, fast asleep. Then I was wide awake. No sound or movement awakened me, but something had changed. The air was different. It pulsed with energy. I looked toward the source of the energy—beyond the foot of the bed, past my feet, and into the eyes of a glowing apparition.

In the corner of the room, luminous in the pale moonlight, stood old Mr. Lindstrom. He was translucent. I could see through him to the silver insulation on the unfinished walls. He wore a somber expression and the dusty overalls he had favored in life, only now they shimmered with a cold bluish hue.

He was so still, beseeching me with sad, serious eyes. He was Jacob Marley without the chains. I felt his grief, and I sympathized, but the predominant feeling coursing through me was panic. I pulled the covers over my head and trembled from head to toe. My heart thumped so hard it moved the sheets up and down and banged in my ears.

"Okay, Lorri, think about it," I reasoned to myself. "Mr. Lindstrom can't be here. He's dead. Besides, he's translucent. I must be imagining things. It's just the moonlight glinting off the insulation. (My dad was never in a hurry to complete his projects. Much to the chagrin of my mom, the upstairs walls at the cottage remained unfinished with the insulation exposed for, oh, around fifty years.)

It took several agonizing minutes, but I got my heart rate under control and dared to peek out of the covers to prove my theory of the Lindstrom effect. He was still there. Poor transparent Mr. Lindstrom was staring at me with those mournful eyes.

I don't know how, but I burrowed under the covers once more and immediately fell back to sleep. I knew Mr. Lindstrom wouldn't harm me, and besides, blankets are powerful protectors. When I woke to the sound of finches singing and the sun streaming through billowy gauze curtains, he had gone.

I wish now that I had been less afraid. Maybe I could have discerned the reason for Mr. Lindstrom's appearance. He had conveyed a somber sadness, but I'd been too young and inexperienced to decipher his message or its intended recipient. Reflecting on his visit now, I believe his presence had been an attempt to express remorse over things left undone and unsaid in this life. Mr. Lindstrom had been worried for his wife. He knew how much she needed him. It's unusual for me to encounter such a sad spirit. Most of the time, love is the prevailing emotion emanating from the being on the other side, although it's not unusual for spirits to tell me things they wish they'd done differently. Whatever the message, the parting gift is love. Mr. Lindstrom's message, too, was loving. He wanted to be sure his wife was okay, and someone knew he cared. He wanted to say he was sorry for leaving her, and for other things I was too young to understand.

I hope he found someone better equipped to pass along his caring apology. I'm sure it required effort for him to gather himself into perceptible form, only to have me hide from him.

In an unprecedented act of trust, I went downstairs and told my mom I had seen Mr. Lindstrom's spirit.

"Oh, I wonder what he was doing here."

Unlike my engineer dad, my mother never questioned my psychic nature. She has a level of acceptance not uncommon in Celtic families. My feisty Scottish grandmother, "Hurricane"

Mary MacLeod, had second sight, as do several of her twelve children—including my mother. Clan MacLeod has stories of the supernatural woven throughout its history, dating back to ancient times. Clan legend tells of an infant MacLeod chieftain who received a magical faerie flag as a gift. The versatile flag, known in Scottish Gaelic as *Am Bratach Sìth*, is endowed with the power to multiply MacLeod warriors on the battlefield and enhance fertility; it also can be used to cure sick cows and bring the herring into Dunvegan Loch. To this day, the flag hangs in Dunvegan Castle, the clan's centuries-old Scottish home and stronghold. A visit there is on my bucket list, and I wonder who and what I'll sense within the walls of my ancestral home.

Like many embattled Highland clans, the MacLeods' is a bloody history. If you're a fan of Monty Python, you'll remember the Black Knight—an unstoppable warrior who loses his legs in battle and proclaims it "just a flesh wound." The tale unwittingly mirrors an actual MacLeod battle legend. MacLeods possess an extraordinarily high pain threshold (perhaps owing in part to our fondness for the healing elixir). I plan on enjoying a shot of healing elixir before my visit to Dunvegan Castle. My ancestors are not shy. I'm prepared to be tackled.

Just like flamboyant red hair and disinclination for temperance, psychic intuition is an inherited trait characteristic of clan MacLeod. Perhaps one day, we'll find the DNA strand responsible for its transmission. Hurricane Mary had intuitive dreams and visions. Her daughters—my aunts—also have premonitions and psychic dreams. One aunt dreams of snakes before hearing of a death in the family. Other family members have a psychic connection to animals like I do with red-tailed hawks, crows, and toads. My sister Mary is visited by a hawk, our mutual spiritual compadre, whenever I'm having an emotionally charged day. She calls and asks, "What's going on? A hawk just landed in the back yard and stared right at me." Each time this happens, I'm either thinking of her or in a moment of connection with the spiritual side.

The bond with toads fascinates and amuses me. I can't explain it. Spirit animal guides are an accepted part of many cultures, so I roll (and fly, and hop) with it. Do others in your family have premonitions or bonds with certain creatures? Has the topic ever come up? In my family, there are similarities in the nature of our experiences. Premonitions and psychic dreams are most common. You may find the same is true in your clan. If you have a close relative who feels a connection to animals, this may also be true for you. If you've never discussed intuition, don't assume it's because no one has it. Be the first to broach the subject, and see what's revealed.

# Dream Visitations

My great uncle died the year I turned sixteen. He was the second ghost I saw, but unlike Mr. Lindstrom, Uncle George appeared in a dream.

A brief history: Uncle George and his wife, Doris, lived next door. They were a loving, gentle couple who couldn't have children of their own. We were their surrogate grandkids. George and Grampa Pete were brothers. George and Doris were the yin to my family's boisterous yang. Their house was an oasis of calm, fragrant with blossoming flowers and plants. Doris had the countenance of a serene Buddhist monk, although she'd scoff at this description if she were alive. She resonated serenity. Wild creatures sensed it and didn't run from her. Birds flitted around her the way they do Disney's Cinderella.

Uncle George was a soft-spoken man who loved beagles, gardening, and his prize pigeons. When he smiled, his blue eyes twinkled. He loved to laugh. It was a special treat when he let me hold the newly hatched chicks in the pigeon coop, a wooden outbuilding the size of a small garage. The light was soft inside, filtered with dust motes and miniature down feathers hovering on gentle currents created by the fluttering nesting fantails and white cumulets. Clean wood shavings covered the floor and muted sounds within. A pleasant, earthy smell lingered in the space. It was like entering another world. Uncle George and Aunt Doris had a gift for making an ordinary suburban backyard into a wonderland.

Like most sixteen-year-old girls with no experience of loss, I understood death only as an abstract concept. Although boys just a few years older than me were being drafted and disappearing into the jungles of Southeast Asia, death kept its distance from my doorstep. Friends, Girl Scouts, church youth group, and school activities kept me insulated from the massive loss of life the Vietnam War was exacting.

I was unprepared when Uncle George became unexpectedly, gravely ill. My family drove up from the Cape to be near Aunt Doris after George's hospital admission. He was diagnosed with acute kidney failure, and I was heartbroken when he died a few days later.

It was a humid August night. My bedroom windows were open to move the stifling air. I woke to a ringing phone—always an ominous sound in the wee hours. It was the hospital, notifying Grampa Pete that his brother was dead. Back in the 1970s, it wasn't unusual for a male relative to be listed as the first emergency contact for a woman's spouse, strange as it seems to us now. It was his terrible responsibility to inform Aunt Doris. He and Dad hastily dressed and walked next door, and poor Doris awoke to a bang on the door that could only mean one thing. I sobbed into my pillow as I heard them through the open window.

It was a somber time. My sisters and I attended our first wake. The youthful illusion of being beyond death's touch vanished, as it eventually does for us all. It felt surreal that I'd never see my dear uncle's eyes twinkle or hear his amiable laugh again.

Three weeks after his death, I returned to high school to begin sophomore year. Heavy grief dampened my excitement. Grief counselors hadn't been invented yet, so I struggled along on my own. Slowly, I adjusted to life's new rhythm and healed.

It was early December when Uncle George appeared in a dream, one unlike any I'd ever had. This dream was more real than waking life, every detail sharply pressed into my awareness. No one thing stood out; every feature shared an equal vividness. It lacked all context. There was just Uncle George in a black coat and fedora, staring directly into my eyes. He held a black wooden cane in his hand. The black of his coat, hat, and cane was darker than any black in waking life. It was bottomless. His gaze transfixed me. He spoke without words. His face wore an ominous seriousness I never saw in life. His eyes held my gaze until there was nothing else in the world, just his eyes burning into mine with excruciating intensity.

I heard a church bell chime three times and knew something monstrous.

I woke up terrified. Somehow, without words, Uncle George had conveyed that Grampa Pete would die in three months.

I told no one about the dream, but I couldn't shake the dread. I went to the calendar in the kitchen and counted out the days until March 10, 1976. I made a tiny dot in pencil on the date. I didn't want anyone to notice the dot and ask me about it, but somehow it felt important for me to mark the ominous day. Was I fearful of losing someone else I loved? Had I eaten too much chocolate before bed? Nothing seemed to explain away the terrible truth I felt. I knew. Everyone was still healing from Uncle George's death. Our grief was still raw. How could I share this terrible knowledge? How could I handle keeping it to myself? I was miserable.

I hugged my grandfather every chance I got. He wondered what was going on and asked, "Why all the sudden affection?"

I couldn't tell him. I teared up and hugged him tighter.

"I just love you, Grampa."

His death three months later devastated me and shook our family and community to its core. He was a rock, a well-loved civil servant, and the stabilizing center of an emotionally volatile family. The town grieved along with us as we buried a jovial, loving family man.

I was heartbroken and angry. I had known he would die, and I couldn't do a damn thing to prevent it. What good was knowing something bad was going to happen if you couldn't stop it? My grandfather had battled lung disease for thirty years after quitting smoking. He had emphysema. He was elderly. His passing was inevitable, yet it came as a deep shock, despite Uncle George's warning. I was angry with Uncle George for alerting me to a tragedy I couldn't prevent.

Now I understand the gift my uncle gave me, as well as the value of being a medium who could receive it. I didn't squander my final months with my beloved grandfather. I cherished every moment we had together. Uncle George gave me the chance to love my grandfather with conscious intention during our final months together. As he lay in a coma dying, I sat by his hospital bed and held his hand. I told him how much I loved him and thanked him for being the best grandfather a girl could have. Although grief tore me with wrenching ferocity, I found solace knowing that on March 10, 1976, Uncle George welcomed his brother home.

# CHAPTER 9

Something's
Wrong With Me

I HOPE NO other young woman suffers the way I did before making peace with her power. By eighteen, I knew something was wrong with me. I was different and not in what I considered a good way. I knew things I shouldn't. I knew what my friends would say before they spoke because our conversations played out like daydreams in my head moments before they occurred in the "real" world. I knew the telephone would ring, announcing choir practice cancellation, moments before the call came. I knew certain people were dangerous, like the new youth minister at church. Everyone loved him. He was so nice. But I felt evil emanating from behind his smiling face. Later he was exposed as a pedophile. Thankfully, I had heeded my inner knowing and avoided ever being alone with him.

I noticed other bizarre qualities, like an ability to absorb technical knowledge through some kind of osmosis. For instance, when I'm listening to an expert discuss a topic I know little about, I'm able to follow along at a level far beyond my education on the subject via what feels like psychic slipstreaming. I hitch a psychic ride on the speaker's knowledge and just float along. It's like I'm channeling his or her intellect, surfing the thought waves. There are times when I understand a foreign language speaker because psychic communication is a universal language.

My sisters gave me the first sign that intuitive ability is not always an endearing trait. They envied the way I found four-leaf clovers, lost coins, and arrowheads by "feeling" their presence. Sometimes it made them cry. Other times it made them hate me, which threw me into conflict. I was the peacemaker in the family. Intuition brought me happy experiences, but it caused tears and bitterness in my sisters. They had no clue how large a burden I carried. They only saw the fun part of it because that's the only part I shared.

Despite my conflicted emotions and certainty I was a freak; there were moments of psychic awareness that shone so bright that all I could do was smile in awe. The bond I feel with wild creatures is the best part of my gift. My funniest creature connection is with the most unlikely of characters—toads.

It works like this: I sense a toad is near. I feel its droll energy. It's as unique as a fingerprint. I look around, and there he is, within a few feet of where I'm standing. I do not understand why I have this kind of bond with toads, but I like it. It makes me smile every time I connect with one. Like their round bodies, a toad's energy is down to earth. For a moment, I get to feel like a toad myself. They don't have many worries. They're like tiny Buddhists, living in the moment, digging the scene.

My favorite toad experience happened in my adult years, on a cold November night, when I felt one in my garage after arriving home from work. It was a raw, miserable night, too cold for any sensible toad to be about. But there he was, a few feet away, crouched in a shadowy corner. His golden eyes were half shut.

He must have gotten stuck in the garage when the doors closed earlier that day. I imagine he'd hopped in when the concrete floor was warm.

Now it was freezing. I lowered my cupped hand and placed it in front of him. To my amazement, he hopped over to my hand and crawled inside my palm. He wriggled his cold belly against my warmth and stuck his head between my thumb and index finger. I held my breath, humbled by the extraordinary experience unfolding and the trust this small creature had placed—literally—in my hands. He gripped my skin with the pads of his chilly fingers, raised up his head, and chirped. I didn't know toads could chirp. To this day, I feel blessed by our moment of interspecies communion. I'm grateful we speak the common language of the Consciousphere.

I microwaved a warm pack and placed it near him on the floor. Then I left the garage doors up a few inches, so he could find his way home after a cozy night's rest. That little toad became a good friend. All the next spring, summer, and fall, he appeared at the back door around dusk and allowed me to feed him bugs, which he took from my hand.

It was a small triumph, allowing myself to celebrate a psychic experience. It was another clue, like finding arrowheads and communing with gentle spirits, that my ability could bring me happiness.

You would think that, as a teenager, I would've been more excited about possessing a super power. There's a reason books, movies, and TV shows about teen vampires, witches, superheroes, and werewolves are so popular. Teens like to imagine themselves as powerful, mystical beings to compensate for the reality that most of us feel like powerless, awkward geeks at that phase of life. I didn't view my abilities as a gift. I took them for granted in early childhood and grew to distrust them when I figured out no one else was having experiences like mine. I viewed intuition through a lens of fear and confusion. I feared I was crazy, destined for a nervous breakdown and eventual institutionalization. No one else I knew could "feel" toads and communicate with spirits. I was a weirdo.

I kept my embarrassing abilities secreted away for years and cultivated a convincing false me to present to the world. False me was normal. She wasn't a shy, insecure girl who had mystical encounters with indigenous spirits. She wasn't visited by the ghost of dead excavators in luminous blue overalls, or deceased uncles. False me was a good actress, but living in the role was sapping extraordinary amounts of my emotional energy. My immune system weakened. I got sick. A lot. My well-being was in serious jeopardy.

I read *I Never Promised You a Rose Garden*. The book's main character also saw visions, and she had schizophrenia, as did my older cousin—did it run in families? One night at the dinner table, my mom told a scary story about a girl in our church who was diagnosed with the illness after putting her hand through a glass window. She had a nervous breakdown. I had a panic attack on the spot (while carrying on as if nothing was wrong). Was I having a nervous breakdown? The phrase shook me. Were my visions part of an imminent psychotic break? I spent exhaustive amounts of energy tamping down my terror of lurking insanity. I hid my nightly panic attacks because I wanted to remain out of the mental hospital for as long as I could. My insanity would embarrass my family. They'd never recover.

For a short time during my early teens, I found solace by becoming a Jesus freak. *Jesus Christ Superstar* and *Godspell* were Broadway hits, and Jesus was enjoying a cultural revitalization.

Since I knew he could keep a secret, I begged Jesus to help me on the nights I lay in bed quaking as waves of adrenaline-fueled panic wracked me. I felt less alone when he accompanied me on my stealth visits to the bathroom, where I threw up quietly so my parents wouldn't wake up and ask me what was wrong. I spent a lot of time in the bathroom with Jesus.

# Psychic Love Connection

The nervous breakdown I was sure was imminent never arrived. Or, if it did, I lived through it. I remained plagued by panic attacks, but falling in love senior year worked wonders for my emotional health. If teenage love was an element, it would be stronger than Titanium. Love hormones bathed me in bliss. I reveled in feeling something stronger than the anxiety that was my near-constant companion.

Maybe this was the answer to all those prayers for help I'd sent to Jesus. One early spring night, my friends and I packed into a station wagon and headed to a dance at a private, all-boys Catholic school. The gym was bright and cheerful, with balloons and boys as far as the eye could see. From across the room, I felt someone's energy attracting me. I looked around for the source and saw a tall, serious boy with intense brown eyes on the far side of the gym. It felt like his energy was boring holes into me. When I met his gaze, something more than physical attraction passed between us. I had the same locked-in sensation I did when I looked into the somber eyes of the departed Mr. Lindstrom and Uncle George, minus the terror and dread. I knew the serious, brown-eyed boy felt it too. We had an instant, larger-than-life connection. This boy was important somehow.

His friend dragged him across the gym to meet me. I felt comfortable with this shy young man, like we were old friends. I'm usually the shyest person in a group, so this was a unique experience. Henry and I talked most of the night. At the end of the dance, we exchanged phone numbers and joined the crowd of kids filing out of the gym. We hugged goodbye, and I rode home on a cloud.

We lived in separate towns and went to different schools, so weekends were the only times we were together. One day over pizza and cokes, I told Henry that when summer arrived, I'd be spirited away to Cape Cod with my family for the season. I loved Pocasset, but these were the ancient days before mobile phones, texting, and social media made communication so easy, and the thought of being so far away from Henry was bleak.

"Where's your summer cottage?" he asked.

"You've never heard of it, trust me. No one's heard of it."

"Tell me anyway."

"Pocasset."

He stared at me. "I live in Pocasset."

"Quit teasing me."

He wasn't teasing. The boy at the dance whose energy had called to me was my summer neighbor in a tiny Cape Cod village. Despite more than a decade of living within walking distance, we'd never crossed paths. We knew many of the same friends and frequented the same small, private beach but had never met. I had a great summer.

Love was a balm that helped me finish senior year with good grades despite my anxiety and occasional panic attacks. Being in love lessened their occurrence, but they'd begun happening during the day, not just at night. Some days started out with an attack in homeroom. Those were long days.

I excelled as a creative writer because my connection to intuition tapped a limitless source of subconscious material. Writing was a sanctioned outlet for my stress. I dreamed of being a satirical writer for the *National Lampoon*, or the next J.D. Salinger. I told my parents my plan.

They were unimpressed: "Writing is not a real major, it's a hobby. If you want our help, you need to choose something that will translate into a steady career and security."

Okay then. If I couldn't be a writer, I'd be a physician. Heck, I spent my days trying to diagnose myself. Anatomy and physiology were my favorite classes—I'd gotten used to the smell of formaldehyde and handling dead cats after the first few sessions. Mr. Pierce, my enthusiastic teacher, gave extra credit if we could extract the cat's pituitary gland intact through the nasal cavity, and I enjoyed a challenge. I'd go to medical school and be a research physician.

"We don't have the money for medical school."

I didn't have a backup plan. It had never occurred to me to go against my parents' wishes. That's not how I was raised. My grades were good but not strong enough to attract a substantial medical school scholarship. I was out of ideas.

I made an appointment with the school guidance counselor. He sat behind a cluttered desk that took up most of the space in a gloomy, windowless office. I didn't like his distracted energy. He flipped through a stack of papers in a worn manila folder with my name on the tab—my permanent school record. He peered at me through heavy glasses.

"I don't know why you don't have better grades in math. Your aptitude testing indicates you have superior skills in abstract reasoning."

Well shut my mouth with a pork chop. He thinks I'm just plain lazy. I'll add that to my "Things that suck about me," list.

"Why don't you be a teacher? Or a nurse?"

Dear God. I didn't want to be a teacher—way too much attention focused on me. Nursing was my only other choice? Nursing required more bedside duties (blood, gore), than medical research would. I got queasy at the sight of blood (our cats in anatomy and physiology class were predrained). My inner voice screamed objections, but I was trapped. False me added another persona to her repertoire—one who didn't mind the sight of blood.

I was accepted into the nursing program of a local university and secured on-campus housing. Dorm life and the rigor of a demanding educational program suited me. Henry attended a different college, and over time we drifted apart as new people and experiences filled the gap.

Hospitals were less appealing to me than classroom learning, which was a red flag since I knew eventually I had to work in one. False me didn't hold up in the operating suite. Real me spent surgical nursing rotation in the bathroom with my head between my knees, trying not to faint. Jesus and I got reacquainted in yet another bathroom as I prayed for help to maintain consciousness and dignity.

Mostly, though, I felt strong and independent as a college woman. I liked my freedom. I liked sharing a room with just one person instead of three. There wasn't time to worry about anything but passing inorganic chemistry and medical microbiology. I was untroubled by scary premonitions or ghosts for a while, until something chilling began to happen.

During junior year, I began clinical rotation with nine other students on a closed psychiatric unit. It was a dark, depressing place. The deinstitutionalization movement in the 1950s had created a population of severely mentally disabled people who were discharged from state mental hospitals but lacked alternative living options. Many couldn't adapt and ended up homeless or back in private mental health facilities. Psych rotation was disconcerting. The male patients leered at our clingy polyester uniforms and made suggestive comments. We cringed at violent behavior, screaming, and fights. I witnessed a male patient violently attacking a catatonic female patient who sat unflinching as he pummeled her head with his fists before being subdued by attendants. Was the catatonic woman was so heavily medicated that she didn't feel the blows, or was her trance-like mental disease responsible for extinguishing normal protective reflexes? The latter possibility reawakened my morbid fear of insanity. Could a brain disorder render one defenseless against attack? I was already frightened by the weird things my brain did. What if it got worse? Would my brain ever make me as sick and vulnerable as these poor people?

There was a handsome young patient on the ward named Joseph. He was a chemistry major who used to go to my university. He was friendly and polite—and not that different from me, which was disturbing. How had he ended up here? Joseph wandered around with a pencil and a pad of paper, writing down equations and formulas. He asked me to help him with the formulas. He couldn't make sense of them. I have no idea whether Joseph's numbers and symbols made sense, but I suspect not. Joseph had schizophrenia. Nothing made sense in his life.

Seeing tragic people detached from reality reignited my fear that I was destined to become one of them. Something unsettling was happening, something I kept hidden. I was having waking hallucinations while driving on the highway from college to home.

As I drove the stretch of highway along Route 195 from southeastern Massachusetts toward home, macabre images of dead women flashed into my mind. I saw purple lips and gray bruises ringed on mottled necks. I saw bodies, naked and stiff, scattered through the woods.

Adrenaline constricted my breathing each time a vision appeared. Why was I seeing these terrible images every time I drove home?

I searched for reason. Was my troubled family history emerging in a visual conversion reaction based on feeling unsafe as a child in a volatile household? (I had no idea what I was talking about. I was grasping for answers.) Anxiety fueled merciless self-interrogation. *What's wrong with me? Am I a deviant freak? Why am I tortured by these horrific images? Does it mean I want to kill people? No! Then why am I seeing these images?*

Desperate to stop the visions, I forcibly drove the troubling scenes from my head by replacing gruesome imagery with soothing themes: fuzzy bunnies, sex, microbiology, the Clash, keg parties. Nothing worked for long.

I confessed to my mom with trepidation. Would she call an ambulance? Was this the part where I'd get taken away in a straitjacket? She was convinced that the visions were psychic in origin and not a sign of mental illness. She suggested I needed more rest—every mother's solution—and reminded me that we descended from a long line of seers. Her mother had seen disturbing things too. One night she'd seen her dead husband standing by her bed. The next day she'd received the telegram notifying her that their son was critically wounded in World War II.

I started to calm down a little. Were my visions psychic, not psychotic?

Mom shared a story I'd never heard. My dad's grandmother had been a spiritualist medium known for boldly announcing the presence of spirits to the living. No filter on this woman's blurting. What a brave soul.

"She died in an insane asylum," Mom added, crushing the brief cheer I felt at maybe not being crazy after all. Later family research revealed that my spiritualist great-grandmother had developed an agitated form of dementia due to untreated diabetes, which was the actual cause of her institutionalization.

I was mentally ill, but not the way I imagined. I was distraught, anxious, and emotionally exhausted. But I wasn't crazy.

It took years to learn the truth about the gruesome images. The visions of dead women reflected a *future* truth, one that was five years away. Between 1988 and 1989, a serial murderer known as The New Bedford Highway Killer strangled prostitutes and substance-addicted women and dumped the bodies in the woods along Route 195. Eleven bodies were discovered. There may be more. The killer has not been found.

I was driving past future graves as the chilling images appeared. Now, as I recall the memory of the visions, my skin crawls. I feel anger for the victims. Why can't I see the name and face of the killer? What purpose do premonitions have if there is no prevention, retribution, or justice?

Then, I was puzzled about how it was possible for premonitions to be disconnected from the construct of time as we knew it. There was a puzzle piece missing, and I was going to find it. Something in me sensed that the answer was within reach. I was right.

The truth about the murdered women empowered me. I hadn't figured out the nature of psychic awareness yet, but I never again questioned my sanity or its truth.

---◆---

# CHAPTER 10

# Metaphysical Detective

THERE ARE PLENTY of books written about mysticism, psychic ability, and the paranormal. If you're interested in conducting further research after reading this book, read *Anatomy of the Spirit* by Carolyn Myss, or *Awakening Intuition* by Mona Lisa Schultz, MD. The late Jonas Salk's book, *Anatomy of Reality: Merging of Intuition and Reason* was a significant inspiration for this book. As I read, I felt Salk's intellect guide me. I sensed his spiritual presence as I wrote, like an enthusiastic coach.

Psychologist James Hillman's book *The Soul's Code*, with its call to resurrect unaccountable mysteries of our lives, is similarly inspiring. Hillman's thoughtful presentation of experiences outside of time resonate with my out-of-sequential-time premonitions. Paul Davies's *About Time: Einstein's Unfinished Revolution* and Jostein Gaarder's *Sophie's World* explore the nature of time and reality. I immersed myself in pondering existence like a dutiful philosopher, confident that the teachings of masters, along with stories by people with mystical abilities like mine, would make things clear. They did. It helps to do one's homework. Don't muddle along for years like I did, wasting time trying to figure it all out on my own.

A colleague I admired told me about a program of study leading to a master's degree in (insert cringe emoticon) metaphysics. What can I tell you? I read the impressive syllabus and enrolled, despite some trepidation about the title. I'll admit that I was reluctant to tell anyone I was studying something as out-in-the-ether sounding as metaphysics. The term gets thrown around in the same circles as fairies, crystals, and unicorns.

One of the first things I learned is that the term metaphysics is in fact mundane, derived from the medieval Latin *metaphysica* and the Greek *ta meta ta phusika*, (the thing after physics), a reference to Aristotle's works, where the books' titles came to denote the branch of study that examined things transcending the physical world.

The metaphysics program was intriguing. I gained a historical perspective of intuition as neither unusual nor rare. It is and has been an accepted and honored human attribute in many cultures, including the indigenous one with which I communicated on the riverbank.

What happened? Why did we disempower intuition? Why are people who discern unseen forces and future realities mocked in our culture? What happened to our wise medicine women, our shamans, our pagan priestesses?

Religion and the scientific age shifted us away from old ways. Much good has resulted from reason-based scientific method— we have cures for polio and some cancers, and we have a greater understanding of the cosmos. In the Western world, we've made admirable medical and scientific advances through the use of the scientific method. But we've forgotten that reason and intuition should work together. As the old-timers used to say, we threw out the baby with the bathwater.

To this day, fear of persecution plays a major role in stifling the expression of intuitive knowing. The shameful Salem witch trials occurred here in my native Massachusetts. I don't have to worry about being burned at the stake for writing this book, but spend time with intuitive women, and you will hear the lingering fear of being labeled witches in collusion with the devil. We know that if we'd been born in a different time, we might have been burned at the stake. We know persecution can endanger us again. Even psychics can't always predict when dark ways will resurface. Jewish cemeteries are being desecrated. Racial profiling is mainstream. It's important to remember that if your kind has been demonized in the past, it can happen again.

There is a fear of powerful women in this world. What better way to keep us weak than to demonize our spiritual powers and minimize our intellectual, emotional, and political strength? Feminine power is an emasculating threat to weak men. Intuition is our superpower. Ridicule is its kryptonite.

As we've seen, the study of intuition isn't suited to traditional scientific research methods. It's not measurable the way tangible entities are. As a result, Western medicine tossed out millennia of ancestral healing knowledge. Look how long it took the ancient healing practice of acupuncture to be accepted in the West. Some medical doctors don't believe that the human body has energy channels through which life force flows. Western medicine's disparagement of intuitive energy has weakened the profession and is complicit in intuition's cultural decline.

We don't call ancient healing "medicine." We call it alternative or complementary, the implication being it's secondary to real medicine (pharmaceutical-driven allopathic health care).

Intuition informs energy medicine to a far greater degree than it does allopathic care. This is one reason we feel so vulnerable in traditional doctors' offices. The intuitive connection is missing. You sense it right away. It's why you feel anxious. Anxiety is intuition's hint that you're not in a safe environment conducive to mind/body healing. You're a slab of meat, and you're about to get poked and prodded with no respect for your higher being. In order to protect professional and personal boundaries, physicians learn to think of patients as "the other." This is foolish—we are all connected, and acknowledging our connection is the most potent medicine of all. A physician with good bedside manner intuitively senses and connects with your humanity, and you feel it.

If you find a compassionate physician who gets that we're radiant, physical and spiritual beings, good for you. Hang on and hope your doctor doesn't retire before you die.

Intuition is enjoying a mild reprieve thanks to quantum physics and fuzzy science, which concedes that observer and reality intertwine in curious, heretofore improbable ways. This is sparking discussions that force philosophers, physicists, and cosmologists to become strange quibbling bedfellows. It's all good. The more we debate, the more likely it is that intuition will reclaim its rightful place in our lives.

That a course in metaphysics is filling up with students year after year is another encouraging sign of change. When I finished my master's program, I stood in my kitchen, filled with excited righteous intention. I was a born-again pagan. With feet planted in earth energy and hands lifted to the heavens like a southern preacher whipping up a crowd, I cried, "Bring it!" And sweet baby Jesus, it got brought. Intuition rained down on me like locusts.

I wasn't aiming for locusts. But you take the good with the bad.

The first sign that the Consciousphere had heard my "bring it" request wasn't easy to bear. Whenever I read or heard about an unsolved crime in the newspaper or on TV, I saw terrible details associated with the event. It was the dead women on Route

195 all over again. Shortly after I made my request, a boy went missing. I had young sons of my own at the time, so this news was particularly unsettling. Frightening visions of the missing child appeared in my mind. He was being drowned by another boy, who later stuffed his lifeless body into a trash bag. The images I saw made me ill and tortured me until I couldn't sleep.

The child I had seen murdered was found several days later in the closet of a neighbor's home. He had been drowned and stuffed in a trash bag. A neighbor boy had confessed to the murder. I felt queasy at the thought that I had some kind of obligation to report myself to the police as a psychic witness. That was way outside my comfort zone. I imagined my Grampa Pete chuckling with his police buddies down at the station if that kind of call came in. They'd joke about the looney psychic lady. I thought about my parents and how embarrassed they'd be to know I was speaking openly about being a medium. Psychic stories were for family, not for parading in public. I thought about the looks I'd endure if I told a disbelieving detective. I would be publicly shamed.

Besides, what good was information after the fact? There was no need for me to confess. The killer had been caught.

What then was I supposed to do with this uninvited information? I assumed there was an expectation of me, but I wasn't sure what it was or if I was up to the task.

There were pathetic "why me" moments where I longed to be an average person without a lick of heightened intuition. I lost my "bring it" mentality under pressure. Who wanted to see this kind of evil? Not me, no thanks. I couldn't—and still can't—even watch horror movies. I can't look at human or animal suffering without experiencing anguish. I look away from nature shows when the lion takes down a gazelle.

I quieted myself the way I learned in metaphysics school and looked within for an answer. The knowing came. Peace replaced anxiety. I needed to accept my knowing without harsh judgment, without analysis. I would see bad things, but I would also know beauty and the serenity of connection with the Consciousphere. I needed to trust that whatever happened, or didn't happen, was what was meant to. I was strong enough.

This was another turning point. My first step in empowering intuition was to stop thinking I was crazy and believe in my gift. Now it was time to add patience and faith to the learning journey. I would travel this road and let it take me where it would. I would experience the transformative healing only attainable by enduring pain and uncertainty. As Robert Frost wrote, "The best way out is always through."

**CHAPTER 11**

# Intuition will Change Your Life

BEING OPEN TO change and all that life wants to teach you is necessary for intuition to flow. But that's easier said than done. When we're filled with the noise of anxiety, fear, worries, and other distractions, intuition must shout to be heard. Once you still yourself, you will hear a calling. Mine told me it was time to make some changes.

Accepting my authentic psychic self meant facing up to all the parts of me that were false. There were lots of them. This was the most difficult part of my transformation from a reluctant medium to a happy one.

My psychic shakeup led me to end a ten-year marriage that was weak at its core. It wasn't a bad marriage, but it wasn't good, either. It was an old story—he was emotionally reserved; I simultaneously needed and feared intimacy. My true self is a bohemian writer who worships nature, spirited philosophical conversation, and wild flights of meditative thought. I wasn't where I was supposed to be. I didn't know where my home was, but it wasn't here in this pretend life I'd made. My husband liked fake me— a yuppie Barbie doll who made few demands, dressed conservatively, sipped chardonnay, and didn't talk about ghosts—he wanted the woman who had walked down the aisle with him in place of the real me. Eventually my loneliness grew intolerable. I felt immensely guilty that I was tearing apart a family, but reconciliation was not an option in our case. We were strangers to each other, and I knew that nothing was going to change that. I belonged somewhere else.

My parents were furious at my decision to leave the marriage. My actions caused them to lose face. In another culture, they'd have been obligated to kill me. They assumed I'd lost my mind, leaving a perfectly good man and traumatizing two children in the process. Their attitude was, "How dare you do this to us—and to your husband and kids?" My guilt was a constant, heavy companion. Any loving support I had hoped for was absent; it had been a conditional commodity all along.

What a paradox. All those years when I'd thought I was crazy, my mom had talked me out of it. Now that I was finally allowing intuition to guide me through painful but affirming life changes, I was labeled crazy. In truth, I'd never felt surer of myself, even though it was beyond painful to be the source of others' pain. I was that desperate to escape and live my truth.

When you let intuition guide you, be ready for the consequences. Maybe your changes won't be as drastic as mine, but even small changes demand a period of adjustment. Surround yourself with support and love. Seek out your real friends. Avail yourself of supportive counseling. Journal. Do whatever you need to do to support yourself through this period of reclaiming your inner knowing. And stand strong in your truth.

Truth is not a halfway proposition. As my marriage was dissolving, I also divorced the two business partners I'd invited into my firm. You may rightly ask where my intuition was when it came to choosing business and life partners. It was where it had always been, in a dark corner like the cold little toad in my garage, waiting for me to embrace it. Without it, I'd chosen poorly. I'd brought the wrong people into my vision. I was proud of what I built, and it was painful leaving behind my dream. There would be lean years ahead as I rebuilt. I sold my shares and began anew, freeing myself from negativity, deception, and ruthlessness. Now I see conniving and disagreeable people as teachers. They show me the beauty of my integrity, compassion, and conscience. Their darkness is necessary to see my own light. Without the lessons I've learned from bad people, I would never have reached the state of happiness, abundance, and contentment I have now.

I was now blissfully free to do something completely different with my life. Guided by intuition and reason, I was seeing the world and my path within it much more clearly. My pharmaceutical consulting work had led me away from my true calling to be a compassionate agent of healing. It was risky to abandon a lucrative business career to start a new path, but trusting intuition, I did it. I enrolled as a student in a program sponsored by Muscular Therapy Institute (MTI), a therapeutic massage school in Cambridge, Massachusetts. As a registered nurse, I was able to progress through the program at an accelerated pace. I'm licensed to practice therapeutic bodywork under my nursing license, but the extra training brought new skills and insights. At last, I was surrounded by kind, intelligent people who took intuition in stride! In fact, intuition is acknowledged as a gift that informs bodywork practice.

I learned to feel energy (or chi, as it's also known), to assess areas of need through detection of subtle fluctuations in its flow. This was my first formal training in seeking out energy messages.

Up until now, messages had found me. Now I was seeking them out. I liked the feeling of added control this gave me.

If you were outside the classroom looking in as I learned to feel energy, you would have seen a dozen people acting like they were playing invisible accordions. The instructor showed us how to gradually bring our hands together until we felt a springy "something" in the wall of air between our palms. Try it—it works. There is indeed a feel to energy. Once you get the knack, you can pass your hands over a body (including your own) and feel the dips and flares that correlate to underlying issues of depletion or excess.

After completing my training, I founded a holistic health practice. I named it Vital Touch Center for Healing. I was part of a collaborative of healing practitioners housed in a serene space bathed in natural light and infused with quiet energy. I met kindred spirits, including holistic physician Nirtana Gloria Deckro, colleague of Herb Benson, MD, who wrote the national bestseller *The Relaxation Response*. His work brought Western scientific validity to ancient meditative practices. Today, the Benson-Henry Institute at the Massachusetts General Hospital continues to teach people how to use relaxation response to counteract stress and build resiliency.

Our healing collaborative taught resiliency through use of holistic psychotherapy, reiki, acupuncture, shiatsu, craniosacral therapy, reflexology, chiropractic, and yoga. I conducted therapeutic massage classes and practiced reiki and massage. I thrived in the new healing space. I even did some public workshops—yes, that's right: introverted, shy me stood in front of a room full of strangers and talked about the value of therapeutic touch. My passion replaced fear, and people actually liked my talks.

I supplemented my income as a school nurse. My new life gave me the ability to spend more time with my sons, and the new balance brought the unexpected gift of abundant physical and creative energy. It turns out that being honest with yourself about who you truly are and what you truly need does that. You find yourself filled with more energy than you ever imagined possible. What will you do with your new energy?

Helping people heal through therapeutic massage was gratifying work. And because I was connected to my truth, a remarkable new intuitive skill was revealed.

**C H A P T E R   1 2**

— ✼ —

# Stories in the Skin

THERE'S A SAYING in bodywork circles: your biography becomes your biology. It's true. We hold our emotions and experiences in our physical bodies—we have issues in our tissues.

Old patterns etch themselves into our neurobiology and literally become part of us until we write a new story. Genetics play a role, but the degree to which a genetic trait manifests, if at all, has much to do with emotional resiliency, adaptability, and our inner state of serenity or upheaval.

It's easy to perceive how our biographies and associated stressors manifest as muscle tension and fatigue, especially for those who grew up in volatile situations where it was necessary to remain on guard in a chronic state of hypervigilance. But I had no clue that it was possible to actually see energetic memories spring into focus when I placed my hands on a person's body. The body holds memories like movies that can be viewed by intuitive people. The first time I touched someone and a vivid image sprang into my head, I was incredulous. I felt like a monkey hearing Mozart for the first time.

I begin each therapeutic massage session seated at the head of the treatment table. A drape (usually a sheet and light blanket) covers the client's body from just below the armpits to the feet. Some therapists use different positioning to begin a session, but this is my preferred technique.

I place my hands on each side of the client's head for a moment to allow them to settle into the experience of my touch and for me to experience their unique energy. Everyone's energy stamp is different.

A pregnant woman's energy vibrates and whirls with the busy intensity of creation—truly an exciting thing to experience. A grieving person's energy is thin and reedy, as if the spirit has trailed off, following the departed loved one to another place and leaving the body depleted. Grieving people need help to acknowledge this state and learn how to call their spirits back.

A dying person has two distinct forms of energy. First, there is a weakening of the physical body's vibrations. It feels like a garden in November: life has gone dormant. Another energy hums in the background, a steady beckoning on the periphery that slowly draws the spirit like the moon draws the tide. It's the deepening connection to what comes next. It feels like being called home. One tide recedes as another floods.

The following are true stories from my therapeutic massage/psychic medium practice. All names and some occupations have been changed to preserve patient confidentiality.

## Thelma

Thelma was a woman of a certain age with a long career as a local TV anchorwoman. She was the impetus for my first channeling experience as a medium. Thelma's adult son Bob lived in a nearby town. After trying unsuccessfully to reach him by phone for several days, she drove over to his apartment and let herself in. She found her beloved son dead in his bed, where he had apparently passed in his sleep.

Overcome with grief, Thelma sought healing bodywork several weeks later. As I placed my hands on her, Bob's spirit careened into my awareness with tremendous force—no subtlety with this guy. Panicked at first by this invasion of my being, I quickly got it together and felt angrier than scared. "Back Off," I said (with my psychic words, not my actual vocal cords). I held up a psychic hand in the universal stop position and held him at arm's length. All the while, I continued to work on Thelma. Remember, I was the girl who could have a full-blown panic attack while allowing me to continue smiling and carrying on a pleasant conversation. So a spirit was invading me for the first time. Meh. I've had worse.

I got Bob under control by demanding that he stop pushing at me so aggressively, or I wouldn't tell his mother he was here. Only then did I tell Thelma what was happening. She'd been a regular client for a while, and she was an open sort of person, so I felt she'd be okay with my sudden reporting of a paranormal event. For the first time, I used the words that would become my go-to introduction:

"I know this may sound strange," I began, "but I have intuition, and right now I need to tell you that Bob is here." At that point Bob held out a ring and showed it to me (actually, he shoved it under my nose). "He's showing me a man's ring, a college ring. He's holding it and shaking it in front of my face. He wants you to know that he's showing me this ring. Does this mean anything to you?"

"Oh," she said, taking my words in stride with a calmness I certainly didn't feel. "I've been wearing his college ring on a chain around my neck ever since he died. This morning, I took it off and put it in a drawer. I guess he wants me to put it back on!"

Bob took it down a few bars after I told Thelma he was present. The last thing he sent through me was love. A tragically sad feeling washed over me. Instantly I knew that Bob had been severely depressed and had overdosed. I didn't share that part with Thelma. She probably knew anyway, and I was too new at being a medium to know how much to share.

"He's so sorry he caused you pain, Thelma. He knows you loved him. He wants you to know that he loves you." Thelma sighed deeply. "Thank you. I knew I'd feel better after I saw you."

I don't think Bob cared whether or not Thelma wore his ring. I believe the ring was his way of verifying for her that it was truly him and not something I was inventing. Spirits often show me an object that is a meaningful symbolic token of their relationship with the loved one they're reaching out to touch. A father who loved to garden will show me his prize tomato. A mother will show me her round pearl pin that her daughter now wears.

## Paulo

Paulo had never had bodywork before. He was a quiet guy in his fifties, a tradesman with rough hands, thinning hair, glasses, and a shy demeanor. He came in because he was having severe shoulder pain.

As I began to work on Paulo's shoulder, the image of a panicked young boy flew into my mind. It was Paulo's little brother. I saw his brother struggling in the frigid waters of a frozen pond. Paulo, just a boy himself, was frantically trying to pull his little brother out of the water. The empathic grief of the experience flooded me. I knew instantly that Paulo had not been able to save his beloved brother.

Would I scare this shy man if I mentioned what I was seeing? What if I was wrong? My brief worry was instantly replaced by an overwhelmingly urgent command to share the vision.

"Paulo," I began, practicing my opening statement again. "This may sound strange, but I have intuition. It runs in my family. Sometimes when I'm working on people, I see things—images of events. If you want, I'll share what I see. If you don't want me to, that's okay too."

He said yes. No one has ever refused, because the receiver is a critical part of the experience, and I would not be able to do what I do without a willing sender and receiver.

I described what I was seeing. Paulo confirmed that his brother had drowned when they were children. He carried the guilt and grief in his body still, because he wasn't able to save his little brother that tragic day. When I touched his painful shoulders that still carried that terrible burden, the wound was revealed, along with his brother's message of forgiveness and mercy.

## Tanya

Tanya's brother Carlos appeared on the scene with less gregariousness than Thelma's son Bob. Carlos didn't burst through the door, so to speak. He hovered on the sidelines, emitting a sparkly light that reminded me of the little stars that dance around Tinkerbell's wand. His energy was light and artsy. Tanya missed Carlos desperately, the way you miss someone with whom there's much unfinished business. He was a troubled man, and their relationship in life had been conflicted. She felt him like a wound.

Because he was polite, and I was getting more comfortable with mediumship, I let him talk through me. I actually let him borrow my vocal cords—just sort of let him take the driver's seat and moved over so he could drive. He told his sister how sorry he was for how he behaved in life. He told her he liked to visit her, that when she thought she sensed him, she was right. After a few sessions with visitations from Carlos, he withdrew. I explained it to Tanya this way: he'd said what he needed to say, and now he had moved back into the All. Even though we no longer have our physical bodies in death, our unique consciousness remains and can be transmitted or channeled to our loved ones through a receptive medium. After the communicated information has been received, our uniquely recognizable consciousness from human life merges back into the collective Consciousphere again.

# Olga

Olga was a Russian war bride who had immigrated to the United States with her GI husband after World War II. One day, she was talking with me about her life as a child in war-time Russia. As she told the frightening story of her escape to the United States to live with her husband and his mother, she handed me a nursing pin that had belonged to her mother-in-law. She asked me if I felt anything intuitive when I held it.

I did. I saw the woman who wore the pin, as clear as if she was in the room with us! This was a surprise to me. Our conversation follows:

"Olga, was your mother-in-law petite but incredibly strong?"

"Ya! Ya! That's her!"

"Olga, your mother-in-law was a hell-raiser!" I actually saw her drinking—a lot—and partying with a bunch of friends, but I didn't say so, in case Olga didn't know that side of her. I didn't have to worry.

"Ya. She had a big problem with alcohol."

Later as I worked to release the tension in Olga's neck and shoulders, I saw dark energetic shadows of abuse. I knew she had been molested by her stepfather. I didn't mention it, but the knowledge informed my work with this fragile woman. In later sessions, she disclosed that she'd endured years of abuse at the hands of that sick man. Sadly, she'd gone from the frying pan into the fire when she married a man who was eventually revealed as a pedophile. Bodywork was Olga's haven, where she was able to release the grip of physical and emotional pain and feel safe.

## Sue Ann

As I worked on Sue Ann's face and massaged her ears, I saw a large black dog affectionately licking those same areas on her body. I also felt great waves of sadness trapped in her tissues. It was our first session, so I waited to share what I'd seen until we were finished.

"Sue Ann, I don't know how you feel about intuition, but I have it. Sometimes I see and feel things when I'm doing bodywork. I felt something when I was working on you. If you want, I'll share it. If not, that's perfectly okay too."

Sue Ann enthusiastically asked me to share what I'd experienced. I asked if she owned a big, black dog. She did. From somewhere outside of myself, the following statement flowed:

"My sense is that it's very easy for you to give and receive love from this animal...easier than it is for you to give and receive it from people. I also get the sense that you really need a good cry!"

At that, Sue Ann burst into tears. She'd been having a rough time lately, and she was lonely. Everything I'd seen and felt was correct. We ended up laughing at the happy coincidence that we'd met and had the chance to share this amazing experience.

# Mandy

Mandy, a straitlaced tax attorney, came in for a relaxation massage. It was tax season, and she was buried in work. As I massaged her hands, a wave of pure sadness and love flowed out of her and into my awareness. It was an aching, longing sadness, so intense that I almost cried. The anguish overwhelmed me, but I knew the feelings were empathic. They belonged to her, not me.

I saw her hands as she struggled with a girl. It was someone she loved, and it was intense. She was afraid for this wildly upset girl, and sadness consumed her. Mandy was a new client. She didn't present as someone who'd be open to intuitive readings. She was a serious, super left-brain person. I worked up the nerve to explain my abilities to her.

"Mandy, do you want me to share what I experienced?"

"Sure."

Her face had a blank expression. Any pain or grief she felt was masked. I shared, as she sat rigid in her chair. She was silent for a long period. I waited quietly, nervously wondering what was going to happen next. Judgment? Anger?

Her face softened. Then she spoke, with heartbreaking sadness, so quietly I had to lean in to hear her.

"Last night, I had an argument with my daughter. She has schizophrenia. She was threatening to run out into the busy street, into the traffic, to kill herself. I was holding onto her with all my strength to keep her from running away. It was terrifying. I was afraid if I couldn't hold on…if I let go…I would lose her forever." She began to cry.

Mandy's experience had settled into her body—specifically, into her hands. It was knotted up in there, and when I released it through healing touch, the energy flew out and into my awareness. The ethereal body, the energy part of our being that extends beyond the parts we see as matter, is a map. I am able to read the energy map emanating from the ethereal body, more evidence that we are connected in invisible yet tangible ways.

# Norma

Norma was a tall, angular woman with large dark glasses and coarse, geometrically cut black hair. She exuded a severe vibe that intimidated me a little. She reminded me of my crotchety third-grade teacher, Ms. Serinski. Norma wasn't the kind of person who invited talk about cosmic or otherworldly matters. It was her first visit to my practice. As she sat in the reception area completing a new client questionnaire, a vision of a dark, muscular man I knew to be a gardener flashed into my mind. The vision was so powerful that I blurted, "Norma, who is the gardener?" Oops. The words fell out of my mouth without the usual warm-up speech.

Trying to recover my cool, I said, "That must have sounded odd. Sorry. I have intuition, and I just had a very strong image of a gardener. Does your husband garden, or work outside?"

"No. Neither I nor my husband ever go outside."

Wow. Okay.

Norma left to use the restroom down the hall, and I let out a breath I didn't know I was holding. I'm learning to trust my intuition, I reminded myself. The only way I'll learn is to keep on testing it. Even if it makes me nervous around people like Norma. I knew by now that if I could read her, then a part of her was open. Besides, she had come for bodywork—she must have been comfortable with some degree of vulnerability.

While she was out of the room, I saw the gardener again, this time in more vivid detail. He was attractive, a stocky, gray-haired man with the musculature of someone who's worked at hard labor all his life. He was Italian. His hands were gloved, and he was pushing a wheelbarrow down a steep slope away from the high stone foundation of a gracious home. There was a cellar door cut into the foundation. Above the cellar door, another door exited to a deck.

When Norma returned from the rest room, she said, "I just remembered while I was in the bathroom. On the way here, I was thinking about calling our gardener, Leo." I asked her if he was a gray-haired man of Italian descent. I described the house.

"Yes, that's my house. That was Leo," she said matter-of-factly.

Intuitive knowledge doesn't always contain an easily interpreted or profound message. Its meaning isn't always apparent to me because I'm just the messenger. My role is to convey the vision content I am given. It was up to Norma to decipher.

The gift of this experience is that it gave me an opportunity to trust myself and corroborate my vision with a prickly person like Norma.


## Sue Ann, Revisited

Sue Ann, the woman with the dog, returned for another session. This time she asked specifically if I had any more impressions about her dog.

This was a good exercise. It was one of the first times I was asked professionally to actively seek information rather than just receiving it spontaneously. I focused my thoughts on her dog. I tried to "find" her with my inner eye. Until now I didn't know I could search around the energy that connects us for a "hit." I looked into the mist, and sorted out all the bits that weren't Sue Ann or her dog. Then I found what I needed. The images came. Sue Ann's dog was sick. I saw her curled up in a ball and sensed that she had a sickness in her belly. I didn't feel like it was anything dire, but I was still reluctant to share the vision, given what I knew about Sue Ann's attachment to her pet. I didn't want to make her worry needlessly. Careful to use a tone that conveyed concern but not panic, I asked, "Sue Ann, is she all right?"

"No!" she said. "She's sick! She threw up three times today. This is so weird!"

Sue Ann taught me that I didn't have to personally know an animal, or a person, in order to read them. I can "find" information on request. This was a whole new level of awareness of the versatile gift of intuition.

Once I got it that information is available regardless of whether or not a person is physically present, I saw the rationale. Energy, or consciousness, is pervasive. It's everywhere at the same time. There is no "here" and "there" in the energy of the Consciousphere. If a person is in Stockholm, and I'm in Boston, I can still find her energetically and read her. If a person has physically died, and I am in the living world, I can still sense him. Distance is an illusion. The ability to intuit information is not contingent on location. Everywhere is right here, even the place we call heaven.

One day shortly after this revelation, I got a chance to share my new awareness. Patricia, the acupuncturist with whom I shared an office was ending a treatment. She closed her treatment-room door and greeted me in the reception area.

"Lorri, when my patient comes out, I'd be very interested in your psychic impressions about what's going on with her. I know something's off, but I don't know what," she said.

I smiled, filled with new enlightenment and happy at this chance to share it. "Patricia, a door is no barrier to reading your patient. It's just a piece of wood."

I shared what I intuited. Her patient was about to divorce an abusive husband. She knew he was betraying her, and she'd had enough. Although her patient didn't reveal this truth until a later session, Patricia used my reading to inform her work with an emotionally fragile woman.

**CHAPTER 13**

❦

# How to be a Medium

BEING A MEDIUM is like being a fiber-optic cable. Data flows from one place to another through a conduit, hence the use of the term "channeling" to describe the medium's ability to transmit a message from the Consciousphere to its intended recipient.

I'm the bridge. I'm a bigger example of what happens within the brain's neurotransmitter system when it processes information. Neurotransmitters are the fifty or more chemicals that transmit our thoughts and feelings. The neurotransmitters bridge gaps, or synapses, between a neuron's nerve cells (the senders) and dendrite nerve extensions (the receivers). Mediums are just like neurotransmitters. We ferry information across the synaptic gap between the spirit and physical planes. Nature is full of repetitive patterns. It's brilliant, don't you think? Why start from scratch when the same processes work beautifully in many different situations?

Being a medium isn't just about communicating with spirits. I'm a medium when I access any data from the Consciousphere. If you want to try your hand at mediumship, here's a map to get you started.

# Step One: Quiet Your Inner Critic

Let yourself collect data about a new way of seeing the world without judgment. Think of yourself as an eager student. You need encouragement, not criticism.

I feel bad for intuitives who grow up in households with religious beliefs that demonize their abilities. Those poor kids. How is possessing an extraordinary aptitude for intuition different than being musically or athletically gifted? When you look at it this way, it makes you wonder what all the fuss is about.

Social convention discourages use of our "sixth" sense, probably in part because it's not as easy to understand as a knack for sports or playing the ukulele. It's a muscle rarely flexed publicly in our culture, unless it's in the frightening extreme. Consider *The Exorcist*, the film that did for mediums what *Jaws* did for swimming. Remind yourself that intuition is a gift. Believe in your right to be fully who you truly are. Put your intentions into words, and ask the Consciousphere for guidance. Quiet your mind so you're able to notice subtle messages. I know so many people who say they never receive intuitive information. They're also people who spend huge amounts of mental energy complaining, feeling angry, and worrying.

# Step Two: Remember You're in Charge

I don't believe being open to intuitive knowing puts a person at risk of being possessed by evil demons, as some suggest. I think that's just fear and too many Hollywood movies talking.

No one enters my house without permission. Sometimes the person trying to communicate clamors loudly for my attention, like Thelma's son. If you've ever had a toddler repeatedly tug on your leg while droning, "Mom. Mom. Mom," while you're trying to talk to someone on the phone, you know what I mean. It's aggravating. But it's usually not scary.

If you feel a presence that's a little too close for comfort, remember that you're the boss. Like a parent, you need to set clear limits and boundaries. It's not difficult. Just tell your guest to sit tight until you're ready to engage with him or her. You also are entitled to say, "Not now, please. I'm busy. Call me later."

# Step Three: Acknowledge the Triad of Communication (Sender, Medium, and Receiver)

I can't be a medium without a sender and a willing receiver. I can't read you or give you a message from a spirit unless you're open to it happening. You may not be aware that you're open to psychic awareness, but if I can read you, then you are. This is why no one ever says no when I ask permission to share my impressions. I don't *have* impressions unless there's a willing recipient waiting for the intel. I ask to be polite; I already know the answer.

There's a coming together of energy that creates the right atmosphere for a psychic transfer of information. I'm defining energy in this context as an invisible force that unites all things and flows through the body. Some people call this energy "life force," "chi," or "vibrations." Kindred spirits are said to be on the same wavelength. This is an accurate description of how it feels when I encounter someone who's open to transmitting and receiving psychic information. Do you have certain people in your life with whom you feel instantly at ease? You are probably energetically compatible. When I meet someone, I can tell immediately if we're on the same wavelength. I can walk into a crowded room and pick out the people who are "open." They literally feel different to me—more vivid than others, more radiantly present. Their energy hums and dances. Others feel flat in comparison. Since I believe everyone possesses intuition—given that we're all part of the Consciousphere—I think some of us just don't have a clue. People who practice meditation, or who are naturally intuitive like me, radiate their connection to the Consciousphere with greater intensity. We're floodlights in a room full of candles.

When I meet a receptive person, I have a feeling of instant recognition, like seeing an old friend's face. I can't read a person who's not receptive. That's not failure. Don't think something's wrong if you're not able to get a read. Sometimes people think they're ready to hear, but unconsciously they're not. Or you could just be having an off day. Keep at it.

# Step Four: Be Fierce

Some of your experiences will shake you up. Others will bring indescribable love and solace. Some will strip you raw. All will transform you.

I'm going to tell you about a powerful medium experience I had with a woman who reached out to me after she was murdered. I really like her. I wish I'd known her in this life. She taught me that even in the midst of evil, love burns bright. She taught me courage to witness painful things, because in the end, only love prevails.

# Dominique

In May of 2006, I woke in the early hours to the vision of a beautiful young woman reaching out to me. She stood a few feet from my bed, engulfed in flames. She stood calmly, unaffected by the fire. This was not a vision in my mind's eye. I saw her like I'd see you, if you were transparent and standing in my bedroom. She stood serenely, radiating palpable confidence, strength, and purpose. She stretched out her arms to me in a gesture that meant "Look. I have something to show you."

She showed me, in my mind's eye, images like snapshots. There was a parked white van. A city park. Something black on the ground, smoking. A run-down, multiple-family building on an urban street. Then she was gone.

I didn't feel scared. I felt like I'd just been given a really important assignment, and I needed to get it right.

I waited until it was light and got out of bed. I made coffee and decided to be brave and check the news, since I knew there was a story connected to my vision. There she was. Dominique was a popular high-school student from a suburb of Boston. She had been murdered. The assailant had strangled her to death and hidden her body for two days in a rooming house before moving it to a city park where he burned it to remove forensic evidence. That was where her body was found. The TV news story showed the rooming house, which looked exactly like the building Dominique had showed me. Then the cameras turned to the van the murderer had used to move the body. It was white.

The resolve of this lovely, strong young woman resonated fiercely in me. As I watched the news story, Dominique spoke to me. She told me why she had come. She wanted it to be known that she had fought valiantly for her life. She wanted to be remembered as a fighter, not a helpless victim. She had bitten and kicked and scratched at her assailant. His skin was under her fingernails, but he had burned that evidence. She had kicked him so hard that he vomited. She wanted this to be known. She was so much more than a victim, a burnt body smoldering in a city park. She wanted her mom to know how much she loved her. I felt her love for her family as she told me this. It flowed through my body like purity. After all she'd endured, only love remained.

I sat down at the kitchen table and cried. This brave young woman radiated grace and serenity, even after losing her life to a monster. I thanked her for coming to me with her message of love.

I got out a small note card and struggled to write a letter to her mom. I'd never written a letter like this before. I shared Dominique's message—how she'd fought for her life, and how much she still loved her family. I didn't want to cause her mother grief. Would a letter like this from a total stranger distress her? Might her faith view intuition as evil? How would I find her address? Finally, I decided to mail the letter to the police station. I would leave it in their hands to decide whether or not to share it. I hope they did. My fear of publicity kept me from putting a return address on the envelope, but I signed the letter with my first name.

No one ever contacted me, so I don't know what happened to my letter. As I write her story, I feel Dominique's fierce, beautiful presence once again. I asked her to help this book find its way to her mother, if that is what's meant to be.

Dominique helped me understand that every time I channel a spirit, I am meant to share the experience. I will probably always feel a hint of reluctance out of shyness and old habit, but now I always share my impressions with the intended recipient. I'm a medium. My job is to deliver the information.

## Step Five: Get Yourself a Role Model or Three

A close friend who knew of my abilities once told me there was a TV show I had to watch. It was *Medium*, the program based on real-life medium Allison DuBois. I liked Patricia Arquette's portrayal of Allison. She was a normal, everyday person like me. She wasn't out for attention. Like me, she struggled with the burden her aptitude placed upon her. She dreamed frightening things and saw alarming images and was deeply troubled by them, just like me. She had kids and a husband and an otherwise normal, hectic life. Since I didn't have a real-life intuitive friend, Patricia's Allison became my role model for a time and helped me normalize my experiences.

It's good to have medium role models. If you don't have one, feel free to consider me for the position. Use my experiences and advice as your guide. Thanks to the Internet, you can research legitimate mediums fairly easily. If there's a Spiritualist church in your neighborhood, start there. I've found highly compassionate and skilled mediums this way. Some mediums offer workshops and classes. Take what feels right from these workshops, and leave what doesn't. Every medium practices his or her craft differently, and there is not one right way. Not every medium shares the same techniques, dress, religion, or philosophy. It's not a cult. Pick and choose what you want to adopt, and leave the rest.

# Step Six: Practice, Practice, Practice

Practice on nonjudgmental friends. Ask someone to let you read them. Explain that you're in beta test mode and just need to blurt whatever thoughts or impressions come to you. Ask for feedback. Keep a journal of corroborated impressions so you can review when you're at your best as a medium. Do you do your best work when you're outside or indoors? Does music encourage your mind to open? Do you need a prop, like tarot cards, rune stones, or a personal belonging? If this feels too advanced, try just jotting down how strangers "feel" to you. The process of noting your instinctive reactions will help you tune into your intuitive knowing.

How will you know if your awareness is heightened through these exercises? You'll know. You'll receive some corroboration of your impressions. You'll notice synchronicities you've missed before. You may have unsettling premonitions, along with those that predict good things to come. Don't run. It's all part of the package. It's worth it, I promise. Remember, you are not only bringing the gift of heightened awareness and joy into your life, you are elevating intuition to its rightful place and helping guide the evolutionary course of humanity.

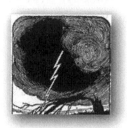

### CHAPTER 14

—— ⌘ ——

# Handling Psychic Warnings

Scary premonitions. Who needs them? They're alarming. Being a medium means you take the bad with the good. Premonitions may be frightening, but they can save your life.

I was living in Boston, on the top floor of a three-story building owned by my fiancé and future ex-husband Paul. One night, I dreamed that a man with a crowbar broke into our apartment. The dream was so real, and so vivid, that its ominous residue lingered long after I woke. It followed me to work, where I told my fellow nurses about it in the break room. It stuck to me, trailing dread with it. I attempted to diffuse some of its power by talking about it in the light of day. It didn't work.

The following weekend the dream came true. Paul and I were asleep. It was a stormy evening, too wild to go out, so we ate in and went to bed early. A few hours later, I woke to the sound of a loud crash and wood splitting. I shook Paul, but he was a deep sleeper. I couldn't rouse him. Great. I jumped up to investigate on my own. I walked out of the bedroom, into the living room, and headed left toward the kitchen.

In the dark kitchen, I almost walked into the man from my nightmare. In his right hand, he held the crowbar that he'd used to smash through the back stairwell door. I feared the next thing he was going to smash with it would be my head. Fortunately for me, he panicked upon finding that the apartment wasn't empty. I guess he'd thought it was going to be an easy heist. He started mumbling, "This is it. This is the one." I don't know whether he meant "This is it, you're about to die from a crowbar wound, lady," or if he meant "This is it, I'm about to be killed by a white lady who wasn't supposed to be home when I broke in." Meanwhile, my fiancé had awakened and was screaming at the guy to get the expletive out. The intruder did leave, after a few tense moments during which he grabbed a cashmere sweater off the back of a chair. I guess he didn't want to consider the break-in a total waste of his time.

After the police left, our downstairs neighbor Bridie delivered a glass of Irish whiskey into my shaking hands. I gulped down the burning liquid. I'd never drunk straight whiskey before. It was a good time to start.

Had I not been forewarned, I might have written the crash off as a tree falling in the back yard and not sprung up to investigate. The intruder could have come upon us in our beds, and who knows what chance we would have had to escape then.

## Warning for a Friend

The following spring, I awoke from a rare afternoon nap. I was having one of "those" dreams, the more-vivid-than-real-life variety. I saw my friend Sarah lying on a slab in a morgue. I felt a sense of imminent danger. At the time, Sarah was living in an apartment in the house beside mine. I woke with a start and immediately ran down three flights of stairs to the front porch. I didn't stop to think where I was going. My legs just took me, and I followed them.

There was a police cruiser parked in front of my house. Two officers held a man in handcuffs. He had been trying to get into Sarah's house to harm her. It turned out he was a man she'd dated; he was stalking her. Fortunately, she was away at the time of the attempted break-in. I told her about the dream when she returned. It was a warning meant for her. She heeded it and eventually moved, changing her name and address in order to remain safe from her stalker.

# Timber!

One brilliant sunny Thanksgiving morning, I decided to take a walk before starting preparations for the feast. I was living in my post-divorce home, a California ranch flooded with light that overlooked a pond and horse pasture. As I started off on my morning walk around the neighborhood, I was surprised by the flash of a vision—a crashing tree—accompanied by an overwhelming urge to protect someone from the impending disaster. I was convinced that a tree was about to fall. I began frantically looking at the root bases of every tree I passed. Then I saw it. It was a forty-foot pine, not fifteen feet from a neighboring house. As the wind caught in the pine's high branches, an area of grassy soil about four feet from its shallow root base rose and heaved ominously. A sudden panicked urge to warn the inhabitants of the house gripped me. I didn't know them, so this was going to be a strange visit.

I ran to the front door and rang the bell. A woman peeked at me through a fancy glass insert in the door, confusion on her face.

Who was this strange, frantic-looking woman ringing her doorbell on Thanksgiving morning?

When she opened the door, I saw a large open foyer where family had begun to gather. The lady of the house invited me in, still eyeing me oddly. As I talked, I gestured to the family to follow me to the side of the foyer farthest from the tree.

"Come this way, please! Quickly! There's a tree in your front yard that's going to fall!"

"Which tree?" asked the woman who let me in. As soon as she uttered the word "tree," a deafening crash shook the house as the massive tree slammed onto the roof. The house shuddered. People screamed. From the open foyer I could see into the upstairs hallway, where a naked man covered in soapsuds was sprinting away from the damage with a washcloth over his man parts. The tree had fallen onto the roof of the upstairs bath, narrowly missing him as he showered.

After everyone calmed down, I looked out the front door. The tree had fallen right where I'd been standing seconds earlier. The woman of the house had been preparing to take her dog for a walk when I arrived. We could both have been struck by the gargantuan tree.

I felt proud that I'd followed my intuition and possibly saved a life or two. I'd stepped way outside my comfort zone by crashing a Thanksgiving gathering—along with a tree.

## Mother's Intuition: The Mother of Them All

When my son was fourteen months old, he became ill. We were in the midst of a brutal heat wave, so at first we thought he was just lethargic from the humidity. But intuitive bells were clanging in my head, and when he started vomiting black bile, my husband Paul and I rushed to the emergency department of the local hospital. After waiting way too long, as people with sunburns and broken fingers were triaged ahead of us, I got up and demanded that my baby be seen immediately. Those clanging bells had turned into deafening gongs. It worked. We were taken to a bay where a doctor examined my son and said, "It's probably a virus. Take him home and keep him hydrated."

"No."

Did I just say that? Me, the people pleaser? Yes, I did.

"You're not a pediatrician. I want a pediatrician to examine him. Something is very wrong, I feel it." Who *was* this woman?

The emergency room doctor was clearly irritated, but he called for a pediatrician.

A calm pediatrician who resonated with healing energy appeared. She carefully examined our son.

"You're right. Something is wrong with your baby. He's lucky you brought him in. I think he has a blockage in his bowel."

A few tests later it was confirmed: our son had a life-threatening bowel obstruction and required emergency surgery. We spent the night at the hospital, in a state of powerless terror only parents of gravely ill children know.

My medical experience helped me recognize my son's symptoms as troubling. But a deep foreboding that transcended all logic governed my actions. If I had taken the first doctor's advice based solely on objective data, our son would have died in a matter of hours. Trusting my inner knowing empowered me to speak up and demand what I knew was needed for my child. Now that sick little baby is a college professor with a scar on his belly where nearly a foot of gangrenous bowel was removed before it ended his life.

It's not unusual for women to have their first encounter with psychic knowing after giving birth. There is no stronger psychic bond than the one that exists in a healthy mother-child relationship. My sons are grown, but I still catch myself thinking of one of them just before they text or call.

As connected as the mother-child intuitive bond is, I'm sad to admit there were times when I didn't have a psychic clue that my children wanted or needed my help. I wish I knew why this was so. It pains me to this day. They had to practically bonk me over the head before I noticed. Intuition has blind spots. It's not fair, but it's true. There are things we aren't meant to know, including things we most wish we knew. We are each on a journey. Maybe there are parts of the journey that contain higher meaning locked within mystery. The larger picture eludes us at certain crossings. As parents, all we can do is constantly reassure our children that they are loved and that we're there for them—no matter what— and hope they believe.

## CHAPTER 15

❧

# Music, Meteors, and Mystery

IT WAS SUNSET in the great state of Florida, and my post-divorce love Ken and I were watching the sky turn pink over Alligator Alley, headed to Marco Island for a week of warmth and relaxation. It was a balmy evening, and we had the windows rolled down. I started to sing a song that was playing in my head, clear as if it was on the radio. It was an oldie, Brian Hyland's version of "Sealed with a Kiss."

"'Sealed with a Kiss' is on the radio," I said to Ken as I reached to turn the dial. It was. That feeling of interconnectedness washed over me like joy.

I hear variations of this story from other people: wild experiences become your norm when you let larger reality in. Have you found yourself humming a song only to hear it moments later on the radio or TV? If so, pay attention. It means you're in the right state of mind to receive intuitive information. Notice your mood, what you were doing and thinking when it happened. These are clues that will help you be more open in the future.

It rained the entire time Ken and I stayed on Marco Island. We extended our stay for three more days, hoping to see some sun. Nope. It rained three more days. The only time we saw clear sky was at night. In a rural coastal area with low light pollution, the stars were spectacular.

One night after feasting at a nearby restaurant, we returned to the beachfront boardwalk at our hotel for a nightcap under the stars. The night air was warm, and the sky was perfect for star-gazing. Ken was getting tired and suggested we call it a day, but I had this *feeling* going on. I felt exhilarated, in a state of great anticipation. It wasn't just the tasty rum drink, either. I was bathed in a beautiful and profound connectedness with the universe. I felt bliss. I asked Ken to please stay outside with me for just a little longer.

Then, the knowing struck me with a surge of elation. "Ken! Watch that piece of sky, right over there. A meteor is coming!"

I pointed to a small section of the night sky. Within seconds, a dazzling meteor streaked horizontally across the space. I felt waves of elation and awe. Oh my God! What just happened!

I felt euphoric. I've come to associate this elated feeling with being connected directly to the Consciousphere, a state of time-lessness. Yes, timelessness. More about that later.

How could I possibly have known that a meteor was coming? How can I know the future in the present moment? If I can predict what's going to happen, isn't the thing that's going to happen happening now?

The implications are mind-boggling.

It wasn't peak meteor season. I know, because my dad was an avid astronomer who taught me all about celestial events. I have happy memories of lying outside on a big blanket with my family on August nights, eating popcorn, and watching the Perseid me-teor shower show.

What are the odds of predicting a meteor's location at the precise point where it's going to appear within seconds? A meteorite doesn't create the kind of frame drag effect that larger objects exert on space-time. Even if it could, humans wouldn't sense it.

English author and playwright Eden Philpotts is credited with saying, "The universe is full of amazing discoveries, just waiting for our wits to sharpen." Amen to that. Let's assume that if a person can hear songs floating through the air without the benefit of a radio, see images jump out of skin, and predict the random arrival of a meteor, the human brain is capable of discerning far more than we know.

## CHAPTER 16

—— ♋ ——

# Sleep and Dreaming: Intuition's Playground

IN HIS BOOK *Anatomy of Reality: Merging of Intuition and Reason*, world-renowned researcher and virologist Jonas Salk writes, "The capacity of the human mind, in sleep as in wakefulness, when in a state to allow the binary system of the subconscious and the conscious mind to collaborate, is probably one of the most important processes involved in metabiological evolution."

In other words, our ability to dream and access subconscious intuitive knowing is critical to our evolution as a species. The subconscious workings of our brain by night are as necessary to our survival as the conscious reasoning governing our thought processes by day.

When we sleep, the brain releases itself from the realm of reason and drifts into the mysterious waters of intuitive awareness. It is in this state that we are most deeply connected to the Consciousphere. Like the sun and moon, reason and intuition provide structure and balance to our days. Some of us connect easily to both reason and intuition during our waking hours. Others ignore the daily nudges from subconscious awareness that hint at a larger experience of reality. But during sleep, even the most stubborn reason dweller is disarmed.

When our body sleeps, the connection to universal consciousness flows freely, unencumbered by judgmental self-talk and the myriad preoccupations that clutter the brain during waking hours. Sleep is the time when the veil is most transparent. It's why Uncle George appeared to me in a dream, when the anxiously overworked reasoning part of my brain was off duty.

Psychic dreams arrive on their own schedule. Now that I consciously invite them, I have far more. As I began writing this book, several relatives from the other side delighted me with a first-ever group visit. Looking rather pleased with themselves for surprising me, Grampa Pete, Great-Aunt Doris, and my father sat around the kitchen table of my childhood. As is usual in visitation dreams, no words passed between us. My beloved family beamed at me from their seats in the tiny kitchen. I was looking into all their eyes at once! They looked directly back at me, feeling directly into me. It was a lovely surprise to be together again after so many years. They were happy I was writing about intuition. Our love was tangible, every bit as real now as it was when they were alive. I remembered the words of a favorite church hymn, the Gloria Patri:

"As it was in the Beginning, and now and ever shall be, World without end! Amen, Amen."

The sound of my own delighted laughter woke me. My book had just received three thumbs up from the other side.

How do you know if you're having a psychic dream or whether you're just in an ordinary dream? Here's a guide. Psychic dream visitations typically have the following eight characteristics:

1. The dreamer has absolute certainty that the encounter is real, albeit happening in a dream state. The dream feels more real than waking reality does.
2. The dreamer perceives the dream as feeling entirely different from a nonpsychic dream.
3. The dreamer is lucid, or aware that he/she is dreaming.
4. Information is conveyed without words.
5. Vivid detail infuses the dream and is typically remembered with extreme clarity upon waking.
6. There is a profound sense of having experienced something wondrous and important upon awakening, often accompanied by awe and lingering residual emotion from the dream.
7. The dreamer wakes with certainty that a message of great importance has been conveyed.
8. If the visit was with a loved one, there is a strong desire to return and be once again in the company of the departed person.

My dad passed ten years ago, but he visits me regularly in dreams. Honestly, we have a closer relationship now than we did when he was alive. Most of the time he just shows up, and we enjoy one another's company. There's no plot. We're just being, together. None of the tense emotions of the living years are present. Only love remains. I enjoy how deeply comforting his visits feel. He's much more relaxed now.

During one dream visit, my dad conveyed a whole bunch of information to me, although not with words, of course. I remember trying to retain it all. Some things never change—Dad was a man with a mind full of technical knowledge that he had difficulty expressing. I struggled to stay in the dream and hold onto the knowledge he was imparting as my brain began to wake. I knew it was very important info. As I shifted back to the waking state, I couldn't recall a bit of what he'd said. Damn, I thought. This was a first. Usually, I remember the message clearly.

I wondered why the wisdom he shared hadn't follow me into wakefulness. I concluded that it was not my failing; his words had not been meant for my conscious mind. He had spoken truths directly to my unconscious because that is where they were needed. He sees a bigger picture from his side of the veil, and I trust him. I have faith that my spirit is following his guidance.

As you were reading the eight qualities typical of psychic dreams, did any resonate with you? Have you possibly had similar dreams that you dismissed? Just being aware that you have the capacity to have psychic dreams can be enough to encourage their occurrence. You don't have to study or try; just open yourself to the possibility and wait.

As I conducted interviews with intuitive women for my book, I noted that dream visitations were a common disclosure. I'll share one of my all-time favorite personal dream visits with you, then we'll hear from some of the interviewees.

# Lost Soul

It was one of "those" dreams: vivid, and without sound or context aside from a single being with his eyes and energy locked into mine. This being was a baby who looked to be about six months old. He looked so vulnerable, sitting there in the middle of nothing. There wasn't anything else except him and me. We were in a place that isn't here, but that led to here. It felt like a waiting area.

He was waiting to be born!

Our eyes were locked. His dark brown eyes sent a message directly into my being. He didn't know where he was supposed to go. But I knew.

"You're Andy's baby. You need to go to Andy!" I communicated back, without words.

This little boy was the image of my cousin Andy. Their eyes look identical. But that's not what made me decide where he belonged. I just *knew*.

Andy is my first cousin on my mother's side. Our moms are sisters, daughters of Hurricane Mary MacLeod. Andy's mom is the one who dreams of snakes before a death.

My cousin's oldest was nearly thirty years old, and his youngest was ten. It seemed unlikely that a new baby was in the plans. Nevertheless, the dream had come to me and had be passed on. I called Cousin Andy. Psychic dreams require no explanation amongst the Clan MacLeod.

"Hey, Andy. I had a psychic dream. Is your wife pregnant?"

Andy laughed. "We don't have time or energy to try for any more kids! Why? What did you dream?"

I told him about the lost baby who had reached out to me.

"I know it sounds crazy, but will you ask her to take a pregnancy test?"

That was bold of me, wasn't it? That's what psychic experiences demand of me. They endow a bluntness that doesn't normally exist in my personality.

"Um, okay. But I'm sure she's not."

"Thanks, Andy. Love you."

"Love you too."

Weeks passed. I wondered. Then I came home to a message from Andy on my voicemail. "Hey, it's me. Nope, she's not pregnant. The test was negative. You better tell that kid he needs to go somewhere else! Love you, bye!"

Huh. That had never happened before. My dream was spot-on classic psychic. All the elements were there. That baby was Andy's. I knew it.

Still, I forgot about the dream until two months later, when Andy called again.

"You're not going to believe this, Lorri. The first test was wrong. She *is* pregnant, and according to the ultrasound, she was pregnant when you had the dream!"

By the time I got to meet my new baby cousin, he was almost six months old—the age of the baby I'd seen in my dream. His mom wheeled him up to me in a stroller. I looked down at the face of the little boy I'd met in my dream and smiled. He smiled back.

"Hello again, Sean Andrew."

He waved his hands for me to lift him up. I gathered him into my arms, overjoyed to be reunited with my little cousin, who had found his way home.

"That's funny," said his mom. "He never goes to anyone."

CHAPTER 17

❧

# Dare to Share

THERE ARE THREE reasons this book is important to you and to our culture. First, we can't live our lives or function optimally as a society while ignoring our innate capacity to live in a heightened state of awareness. Intelligent dialogue about the nature of intuition must occur in order for this to happen, and the sharing of stories is a means to that end.

Second, by demonstrating the prevalence of natural—albeit culturally repressed—intuitive knowledge, we will demystify and normalize metaphysical abilities. Every woman (and man) with intuition should be free to express her (his) truth without fear of ridicule or persecution. Our submerged voices must resist being pushed down. We must dare to share.

And, most importantly, by honoring your intuition as well as your reasoning abilities, you will contribute to the survival of our species and planet. On both a personal and global scale, disavowing the interconnectedness of the human species as evidenced by intuitive knowing engenders peril. We can't succeed in life with half our awareness turned off or discredited as crazy.

We won't treat one another with love and compassion if we continue to believe in the existence of "the other." There is no "other." There is only us. The first step in raising consciousness about our oneness is getting people with intuition to reclaim their gift, dust it off, and wear it proudly in public.

I posted a request for interview subjects on my book's social media page. I was sure there were hundreds of untold stories, kept hidden by fear of criticism or ruined reputations. I hoped people would be brave enough to step up and be counted. Some were. Bless their hearts, they were. I'm honored by their courage and by the trust they placed in me.

Jami was the first to respond.

Jami's a parent I met during my stint as a school nurse. Her kids were students at the elementary school where I worked. She's an intelligent woman—a skilled registered nurse with the blend of compassion and tough love needed to raise well-adjusted kids. Not all the students I met were as fortunate. My intuitive skills were a valuable guide as I worked with the more-troubled children in my care, many of whom carried burdensome secrets.

Like the majority of people I interviewed, Jami's a regular person with a career, kids, stress, and a busy schedule. She suggested I read her blogpost about a dream visit from her Nana. Her honesty shines through her recollection:

It's been four months, but I still remember it. You don't normally remember dreams for this long, but like I said… I'm sure it wasn't just a dream…I come to see my Nana. My sweet Nana, my dad's mom…the one who I stayed with every weekend after Mom moved away when I was nine. The female caretaker who gave me the attachment bond I was craving after the bond with my mother was severed. In real life, I wear her wedding band. I have her rocking chair. I use her baking pans. I keep her memory alive in my daily routine as best I can.

In the dream, she was there, right in front of me. Sitting at a picnic bench. So vivid. So real. So beautiful…I center myself to her presence. As it is in every single dream I've had about her since she died, I know it's a dream…I'm just so happy I get to see her sweet face in front of me and not have it be a memory or photograph. Since I know it's a dream, I appreciate every second of it, and dread the end…the waking up. Every time I see her in my dreams, she doesn't talk, and I never touch her.

That's just the unspoken rule we both understand… until that night. I see her sitting at the table. She's looking away from me, like she often does. I get up close to her and look at her face, her skin. It feels so good, so nostalgic, to be that close to her again. I'm absorbing every part of what I see…her cheeks, her neck, her mouth, her hands. She looks up at me. I'm standing next to her as she's sitting, and she looks up at me, smiling. But unlike her other dream visits, she has tears in her eyes. At first, I can't tell if she's really sad or happy. As I know it's a dream, I can appreciate that this is different than when I normally see her.

Smiling, I take her face, and I cup it in my hands. I've never touched her in my dreams before. This is so special. I'm cupping her chin in my hands, with my fingers holding each cheek. I'm actually feeling my grandmother, for the first time in sixteen years. God, it feels so real! Her eyes are welled with small puddles of tears, but she's smiling. I know I can't talk to her, nor she to me. That's the rule. Touching her grounded me. Amid all the turmoil in my life, touching her made everything bad stop for a few minutes, and I felt lovable again. In my mind, I'm thinking "I miss you so much. What am I going to do when I wake up, and you're not here?" Wow, I'm crying as I type that sentence. She looks at me and doesn't talk...but she thinks something, and I can hear it in my brain. She thinks, "When you think about missing me, just think about the love you feel all around you. That's me. That's my love." I could hear her think that in my head. I felt the emotion of what she was saying to me.

I emerge from this dream hearing a sound emit from my body...like a start of a wail. I wake up to realize she's gone. I'm in my bed, alone.

Except, I don't feel alone. I realize the magnitude of what just happened, and I feel lucky, because I know she just gave me such a powerful message, even though I'm not sure of what it is. I think that's why she was crying. She's sad for what I'm going through because she loves me like no one has before...she's smiling to show me that love and to let me know that she knows I will pull through this and be happy. I'm not 100 percent sure, but I know it's close to that. It has to be, because in just writing and remembering it, tears are flowing...and I feel happy.

Did you recognize features from our checklist of typical psychic dream features? Let's review:

- The dreamer feels absolute certainty that the encounter is real, albeit happening in a dream state.
- The dream is described as "different" from regular dreams. Jami writes, "I'm sure it wasn't just a dream...I'm actually feeling my grandmother for the first time in sixteen years. God, it felt so real."

- Information is conveyed without the necessity of spoken word.

  "Every time I see her in my dreams, she doesn't talk...I know I can't talk to her, nor she to me. That's the rule."

- Vivid detail is present and remembered with extreme clarity upon waking.

  "So vivid. So real. It's been four months, but I still remember it. You don't normally remember dreams for this long, but like I said...I'm sure it wasn't just a dream."

- There is a profound sense of having experienced something wondrous and supernatural upon awakening, often accompanied by awe and intense emotion.

  "I appreciate every second of it, and dread the end...the waking up."

- The dreamer wakes with certainty that a message of great importance has been conveyed.

  "She looks at me, and doesn't talk...but she thinks something, and I can hear it, in my brain. She thought, 'When you think about missing me, just think about the love you feel all around you. That's me. That's my love.' I could hear her think that in my head. I felt the emotion of what she was saying to me...I realize the magnitude of what just happened, and I feel lucky, because I know she just gave me such a powerful message."

- There is a strong desire to remain in the loving presence of the lost loved one.

  "I miss you so much. What am I going to do when I wake up, and you're not here?"

Must a psychic dream contain all these features? Absolutely not. What is compelling, however, is that our psychic dreams are more alike than different. It's a sign that our connectedness runs deep. Like ubiquitous dreams of falling, being lost or pursued, or being in a position of extreme vulnerability (unclothed in public, or a terrified passenger in a driverless vehicle), our dreams harken back to our beginnings as a species. Instinct for danger is hardwired into our genetic code and our collective consciousness. Psychic dreams warn us of dangers and remind us that we are connected in ways we are just beginning to understand.

# Gyneth

I asked my mother to write down her memories of growing up in a family with psychic abilities. I grew up knowing these stories. Here's one I referenced earlier when I introduced Gyneth's feisty mom, my grandmother Hurricane Mary MacLeod:

> Just after D-Day at the Normandy invasion, my mother Mary MacLeod had a dream about my brother Dick who was in the army. She dreamed she saw her husband, my deceased father Richard, whom Dick was named for, in a WWI uniform trying to hold up a troop train when suddenly the train collapsed on his head. She wrote down the date of her dream on the calendar.
>
> Later in June the telegram came that my brother was seriously wounded. No other info. A nurse at the Scotland hospital where Dick was a patient was writing the letters he dictated home.
>
> We knew something wasn't right because Dick was using a scribe. Later on we learned Dick's wounds were all

located in his brain...bits of his helmet and pieces of the bomb that exploded on that street in France had paralyzed him except for the calf muscles in his legs.

My grandmother's late husband appeared to her in a dream, symbolically acting as a shield, as a heavy metal object threatened to collapse on his head. She later learned that the date of her dream was the actual date on which a bomb exploded over her son, seriously wounding him.

My mother shared more dream revelations:

My brother Alexander dreamed that our other brother Norman was also wounded in Germany. Like my mother had, he wrote the date on the calendar and sure enough, a telegram came validating Norman was wounded on that date.

Now here's another. I was away, spending the weekend in New York with an elderly woman who was an upstairs tenant in our Church Street home. There was a big thunderstorm. I woke up screaming and she said to me, 'It's just a thunder storm, it's all right.' I was dreaming of a storm. Lightning struck me and burned my face. I washed the burn with rain water.

The following Tuesday morning, I was back working at the dental office. The dentist was away teaching at Tufts University Dental School. I was sterilizing instruments, cleaning and filling a small apothecary bottle. First you put bits of cotton in the bottom of the jar with small dental pliers and then carefully pour a small amount of carbolic acid in. I wasn't thinking, and I put the carbolic acid in first. Then, with the pliers, I pushed the cotton down through the small neck opening and immediately felt the splash of acid come up and hit the right side of my face and earlobe. I ran to the sink and washed it. The dentist next door called for a cab to take me to the Massachusetts Eye and Ear Hospital to have my eye checked. All turned out well, but the memory of the dream came to me. It was a precognitive warning.

# Beth

Beth, an articulate professional, shared several stories. The first relates to a visitation that encompasses both dream and waking states:

The first summer that I was living in my new condo, I woke up in the middle of the night because I had a weird dream. It was about a guy I dated at the beginning of college. He was standing in the hallway, outside the bathroom door trying adamantly to tell me something. I woke up before I learned what it was.

When I woke, I felt really weirded out, not just weird dream weirded out, but a really odd, on-edge feeling. At that point, my dog Lucy, who had been sound asleep on the bed, woke up suddenly and started looking around... staring out the bedroom door...but she wouldn't get off the bed to go into the hallway. So she's on the bed trying to stretch her neck to peer out the door. Then she starts with that low bark, you know, the 'grrr-rrrufff' bark. Finally, I told her to cut it out because she was really creeping me out! I was still not wanting to go back to sleep because I felt like I really needed to understand something about all this...So, I get up, go to the bathroom, come back to bed, all the while saying repeatedly to myself what was it about this dream that is making me feel so on edge? I started to fall back to sleep when this very loud voice in my head says, 'Because he has been dead since 1991!' When I checked the facts later, this was true. Wow, I do believe I had a visitation, and Lucy saw it. I still don't know what my boyfriend was trying to say.

My hunch is that Beth's boyfriend was just saying hello to a woman he once loved, who happens to be a receptive medium. It seems Lucy the dog is one too. Animals are sentient beings with their own connection to the Consciousphere that unites us all. Why would they not share the ability to see beyond the veil?

One of the most extraordinary accounts of growing up intuitive I've heard comes from Linda, a successful realtor. I'm sure her intuition helps her connect with potential buyers and sellers and is a large part of her success. Some of Linda's reported psychic experiences may strain credulity. In the spirit of exploration, however, we must consider even the incomprehensible. Meeting Linda, you would immediately notice two things: her beautiful smile and her intelligent energy. You would not expect this polished professional to have stories like this one waiting to emerge:

## Linda

Where is the beginning? Sometimes it feels like something between *Ghost Whisperer* and *Close Encounters of the Third Kind* would describe my life. It has been a life that I felt both fortunate to have but so limited in who I could share my reality with. My closest family labeled me crazy…I would have most certainly been burned at the stake in a different time. It started very young with a sense of presence…not sure who they were…behind me…. next to me…especially when I wanted to close my eyes.

I would have sleepovers…friends would giggle in delight as we would each one by one float into the air. Some of the girls would screech because they would see a face of a ghost in a photo on the wall. What they all didn't realize was that these 'games' were my life. Since as young as I could remember, I feared the 'people' or 'person' in my room, at the bottom of the stairs, in the barn…I began to realize they were everywhere. I could often ask them to leave, and they would listen.

I would later find out that my home was originally the home of Levi Long, a coffin builder. Whenever there was a shipwreck off the coast of Cape Cod, the bodies were brought back to Levi's home for him to build the coffins.

I have seen UFOs, had several experiences with seeing orbs, and most recently experienced an entity whose emotions touched me so closely I was brought to tears (empath). Ouch.

I met Linda when my new husband Steve and I were house hunting. Our travels took us to Onset, a coastal village in Wareham, Massachusetts. Onset is a windy stretch of coastline on the opposite side of the Cape Cod Canal, the side we Cape residents call "America."

Linda showed us a stately Victorian home overlooking a marina. It was a life-sized dollhouse, brimming with eclectic character from the grand entry's winding staircase with ornate rails to its gabled peaks. From a living room adorned with crystal chandeliers, built-in corner cabinets, and large bay windows facing the water, we watched boaters motoring past. A lone sailboat struggled to fill its luffing sails as it meandered upriver to Buzzards Bay.

Steve doesn't like old houses. He owns a construction business, so the first thing he sees when he walks into an old house is work. I, on the other hand, love old homes, especially Victorians. Their eclectic architecture appeals to me. I like the creak of floorboards, the smooth patina on worn-wood bannisters smoothed by a century of touch. How many hands glided over the spot where mine now rests? I like the living scent of wood. I love the way light filters through dimly opaque windows and the energy of long-gone inhabitants hovering like dust motes in the silent air.

While Steve wandered around downstairs inspecting walls and plumbing, Linda and I climbed the winding staircase to the second-floor landing. The landing flowed into an open hallway with four, open bedroom doors and a bathroom in view. Something caught my eye near the closest bedroom door. As I shifted my gaze directly to the door, it slammed shut! I was looking right at the door when it happened. Not a breath of air was moving in that house. It wasn't a windy day, as the struggling sailor outside would attest. All the windows were closed. We wondered if Steve had opened a door, causing a draft, but he hadn't.

Honestly, I'm glad this kind of thing isn't part of my routine experience. Telekinesis isn't my cup of tea; I'm easily startled. I don't like sudden loud noises or things moving without apparent cause, thank you. But I saw that door slam itself shut, and I caught a glimpse of someone hovering in my peripheral vision. I had to accept that whether I was comfortable with it or not, the phenomenon was real.

I decided to read up on Onset's history since I was referencing the village in my book. I read that in the 1880s, Onset was home of a summer camp for Spiritualists. They came from the surrounding area to hear mediums communicate with the dead.

**CHAPTER 18**

❧

# Peering Through the Veil

For now we see through a glass darkly; but
then face to face. Now I know in part, but
then shall I know even as also I am known.

—1 CORINTHIANS 13:12

STORIES OF VISITS between earth-bound folks like us and our compatriots, friends, and family on the other side abound. Semantics force me to call it the other side, but I don't think of life and afterlife as being actual sides. Existence is like the Möbius strip—it only appears to have two sides until you look closer and see that it has only one. The two-sidedness of here and there is illusory. The Consciousphere is sideless.

There are, however, places where the veil is thin. Some of these mystical places are physical locations, like the Isle of Iona in Scotland, or Lumbini, birthplace of Buddha in the foothills of the Himalayas. Thin places may also be moments, like those that occur during prayer and meditation.

At times we stumble unawares upon thin places, or gently lean into one as the human body prepares to release us. In the moments before physical death, we hover between our body home in the physical manifestation of the Consciousphere and the energetic home that comes next.

I passed through the veil once and returned with useful data for my quest to empower intuition. I'll tell you all about it, but first, here's a short story about the passing of my maternal grandmother:

Hurricane Mary MacLeod was a force of nature. She was strong, stubborn as an ox, and nearly as large. Good thing, too, because her husband dropped dead in the middle of the Great Depression, leaving her with twelve children to raise alone. My mother, Gyneth, was her youngest, just two years old when her papa died.

To support her large family, Mary worked as a private duty nurse, midwife, and cleaning woman. She scrubbed the floors of wealthy neighbors. She read tea leaves and cards, using regular playing cards as Tarot cards probably because she couldn't afford real ones. The props psychics use hold no inherent power of their own. They're ritual, used to help the medium settle into the right mind space.

In her later years, Hurricane Mary ran a nursing home out of her house, caring for elderly people far younger than herself. She was the sole nurse, cook, and housekeeping department. Her eight daughters helped when they could.

I asked my mother to write about the night her mother Mary passed, at eighty-nine years of age and still sharp as a tack:

"My older sister Barbara was by Mama's side the night she passed. Mama mentioned she wasn't feeling well. Then she said, 'Barbara, your father is in the dining room'.

'Mama, you're talking rag time,' Barbara replied.

'Am I?' Mary said. And then she was gone."

How comforting to know that our loved ones are waiting to guide us to the next part of life. When her husband arrived to take her home, I wonder if my feisty grandmother didn't give him a stern talking-to for leaving her with a dozen kids to raise alone.

My friend Alfred, a physician's assistant, scoffs at stories of dying people seeing departed loved ones in the moments before their deaths. He postulates that a "death hormone," produced by the dying body is responsible for causing such hallucinations. Alfred doesn't believe that the visions of dying persons are real.

I find the idea of a hormone creating a highly specific false experience more far-fetched than the continuing existence of consciousness.

# CHAPTER 19

— ✿ —

# Synchronicity and What it Reveals

BACK IN THE seventies, while my carefree teenage peers threw parties in the woods, socializing and drinking beer, I spent hours in those same woods contemplating existence. It was another way I felt freakishly different. I was supposed to want to party, drink, and do whatever else was happening at those parties I never attended.

I recently discovered I wasn't the only thoughtful, serious kid in my school escaping to the woods to ponder life's questions and mysteries. Just across town, a studious boy a couple of years older than me was doing the same. His name was Bobby. Being a lowly sophomore, my interactions with him were limited to a barely audible hello as we passed in the halls. I thought he was cute, which instantly rendered me speechless. Still, I could feel that he was on whatever unique wavelength I floated on that made certain people feel more real—more present—than others. I knew he was interested in science, because we competed in the same high-school science fair. I had no idea we shared a survival strategy of connecting with nature to escape from stress.

The other kid out in the woods and fields grew up to be one of the world's greatest living scientists. Robert Lanza, MD, is intimidatingly brilliant. With coauthor Bob Berman, he wrote *Biocentrism* and *Beyond Biocentrism*, fascinating science-based studies of the nature of human existence. No wonder he felt different to me energetically.

In *Biocentrism*, Bob writes candidly about the difficulties of his early years. As I read, my eyes teared up in recognition. I marveled at the coincidence that two kids on opposite sides of town could have such similar childhoods and coping strategies. We go through life feeling disconnected as we experience sorrow, shame, and fear when in fact, others share similar private despairs.

As high-school kids, we independently conducted science experiments with poultry in our basements. While Bob was discovering how to manipulate genes in chickens on the other side of town, I was attempting to counter the aggressive behavior of testosterone-injected rooster chicks using calming stimuli (altered light filtration and my own healing intentions). His research led to advancements in genetics as well as global notoriety. Mine led to the conclusion that helping troubled creatures feel better is my calling. My classmate explores the nature of existence with the pure logic of science; I have chosen to tread farther down the philosopher's path.

I discovered another kindred spirit in the writing of Jonas Salk. I've admired Salk's contributions to the field of immunology for decades, but as I read his philosophical essays, I discovered how instrumental intuition was to his research. He routinely approached problems using the lenses of reason and intuition, and we have a vaccine against polio as a result.

I'm convinced Salk's book *Anatomy of Reality: Merging of Intuition and Reason* found me, not vice versa. I realize this is not a logical statement. It's an intuitive one. Once I began researching the subject of intuition, I immediately started noticing validating synchronicity in events like finding Salk's philosophical essays. I discovered respectable writers and scientists who shared my forensic curiosity about psychic knowing. Acquaintances with whom I'd never revealed my abilities dropped the word "intuition" in conversation, many of them people I'd never imagined would use the term.

It's easy to ignore the subtle waypoints that tell us we're on course. Noticing synchronicity is powerful validation that you're awake.

After my father died, I was in a thick haze of grief. Reality literally felt like the misty inside of a cloud where I was wandering, raw and lost. I didn't know what to do or where to go. My grief was all I could feel. There wasn't room for anything else.

I robotically dressed the morning after his death and drove to the train for work. I walked through the streets of Chinatown to my office on Boylston Street, ascended the steps of my building, and got into the old elevator. I got off at my floor, buzzed myself into the restricted work area, and sleepwalked to my cubicle. I sat down and stared at the drab pattern of the blue fabric cubicle wall as if it held some answer.

A gentle voice cut through the fog.

"Lorri? What are you doing here?"

It was my supervisor, Lorraine, one of the most caring, grounded people I know. She sat down in my cubicle. She held my hand and said, "You need to go home."

I retraced my steps back to South Station, inside my personal cloud of grief. I began to worry about myself. Could I get myself back home? I suddenly felt exhausted to the point of collapse. I asked my father to help me. "Dad, please just help me get back home. Don't let me fall asleep and miss my stop."

I boarded a midmorning train I don't normally take. As the door in front of my section slid shut, I saw the number printed across it: 231, the street number of my family home and the address my dad had had his entire life. I felt his loving protective presence embrace me. I slept, but he woke me in time to get off at my stop.

Since his death, the number 231 has followed me and my family members. When I remarried and moved to Cape Cod, the first police cruiser to pass my house was car 231. I avoided a bad accident on the highway by slowing down when the car in front of me did, just in time to avoid a big pileup. The license plate on the car ahead of me read 231. I wake in the middle of the night and notice the clock reads 2:31. I smile and say, "Hi, Dad."

When my sister and I text or e-mail, we often note after the fact that our message time stamp reads 2:31 far more often than could be pure coincidence. Our dad was an electrical engineer. It makes sense that he communicates with numbers.

While writing this chapter, I paused to work on obtaining permission to use excerpts from Salk's *Anatomy of Reality*. The permissions form required me to enter the book's ISBN number. I opened the text to copy the number and smiled when I saw that the ISBN number of the book I had most valued while researching mine began with 0-231.

# ESP

My mom was a fan of George Joseph Kresge, a.k.a. The Amazing Kreskin. In the 1970s, this self-described "mentalist" had his own TV show, *The Amazing World of Kreskin*. He performed feats of

ESP (extrasensory perception) with audience participants. When I was ten, my mom used to encourage my ESP by holding up playing cards with their backs to me and asking me to predict their suit. I was right more than I was wrong, which excited her. She was more enthusiastic about my psychic ability than I was. By then I'd learned to be cautious about sharing my authentic self. Sure, it was fun to please her. But there was a big roadblock to true enthusiasm: I'd internalized the message that I wasn't allowed to behave in any way that might bring shame on my family. Something as irrational as intuition was certain to bring ridicule in its path. It was more than a little confusing that my mom was so enamoured with my psychic ability. Wasn't that something that would draw negative attention? I think the fact that her family of origin took intuition in stride framed her perspective on psychic knowing as acceptable. Still, my ambivalence about second sight ran deep. I wonder how different my early life would have been had I honored and nurtured it within myself.

I didn't want any residual reluctance getting in the way of writing this book. To that end, I worked with Beth, an intelligent, insightful, licensed clinical social worker. I sought her help to quiet the reflexive fear I still encounter when speaking and writing publicly about a subject I've faced with ambivalence most of my life.

I found Beth through an Internet search. I allowed intuition to guide me as I scrolled through dozens of possible candidates to help with my work. I use my intuitive search engine often, with excellent results.

At our first meeting, I discussed my manuscript and my history as a reluctant medium. As I spoke about extrasensory perception, I asked if she remembered *The Amazing Kreskin*. I don't know why the old TV psychic's name popped into my head at that moment. It sounded kind of strange to me even as I said it. I hadn't thought of the guy in years.

Beth interrupted me to ask, "Why did you just mention Kreskin?"

"I don't really know," I said. "He just popped into my head."

She smiled. Not only did she remember him, she knew him. When she was a child, Kreskin had lived across the street from her family's cottage on Cape Cod. She has a photo of herself and her siblings with him, taken by her father. I'd had no idea that Kreskin had lived on Cape Cod. Like I said, I hadn't thought about him in decades and never had a clue about his personal life. The woman I chose to help me empower psychic knowing had one degree of separation from a famous psychic.

There are no coincidences. Beth, a total stranger until recently, believes that intuition is a natural human ability that should be honored, not feared or disparaged. I could not have found a more fitting person to support my work.

I live in a body that operates with a degree of daily pain due to arthritis, particularly in my neck. Pain affects my day-to-day life in a way I wish it didn't, but I deal with it. In the months before I met Beth, probably because I've been sitting at the computer writing so much, the neck pain had worsened. It was wearing me down. I became uncharacteristically weepy when I confessed to Beth that I lived in chronic pain. I normally put up a stoic front when I'm hurting because I have a neurotic fear of being viewed as weak, even though in truth I have an alarmingly high pain threshold. I took ibuprofen instead of morphine after both of my C-sections. Beth told me she'd just completed physical therapy for neck problems and understood personally how exhausting neck pain could be.

Serendipitous commonalities like this tell us we're on the right path. Thankfully, I followed the intuitive nudge that led me to Beth. It would have been disheartening to bare my soul to a new therapist only to learn that she had a religious aversion to the

topic of intuition, or was a disbeliever. That didn't happen, because I listened to my inner guidance system.

One day as Beth and I talked, I referenced a period during my
thirties when I had lived near Boston. I was recently divorced and
consulting with Martha Stark, MD, a brilliant Harvard physician re-
nowned for her cutting-edge work in holistic psychiatry and psy-
choanalysis. Beth said she had trained under Dr. Stark. My mouth
literally hung open for a few seconds.

We agreed that the synchronicity was remarkable. Any one
of the similarities we discovered could be written off as mere
chance; the gestalt was an affirming nod to the larger truth behind seeming coincidence.

# The Goose

I experienced a host of troublesome illnesses and physical pain
while writing this book. The neck quieted down, but a torn me-
niscus in my knee made walking increasingly painful. I didn't let
it stop me from traveling through England, Scotland, and Wales
last summer on a bus tour. I was the youngest and slowest person
in the group. Peer pressure and pride kept me propped up as I
limped my way across the UK.

I gave my knee seven months to recover, and it refused, so I
had a surgical repair. A week after the surgery I got shingles. A
week later, I developed excruciating low-back pain from spending
seven months walking off kilter. I couldn't lie flat, so sleeping was
nearly impossible.

After two weeks, I was sleep deprived and in tremendous
discomfort. I glumly fantasized about remedies ranging from
medically induced coma to medicating myself with a whole plate
of brownies, but ultimately opted to use meditation, ibuprofen,
and decaf ginger tea. I was still pretty miserable.

I went from being a vibrant, active person to feeling like I was a frail senior citizen. My days were spent driving between physical therapy and an aqua arthritis program at the local YMCA. I was the youngest aqua arthritis participant by a good fifteen years, and the slowest. Sound familiar? I was becoming a junior senior. Some of my pool mates were well into their nineties. They inspired me, but it was depressing. I stood in the tepid water making wrist circles and gazing dejectedly through the glass panel that separated us from the Olympic-sized pool where younger, stronger people were swimming. For just a moment, I succumbed to tears. I figured no one would notice with all the splashing going on.

I had swum competitively in high school. Now look at me, I thought. Instead of zipping down the lanes with taught muscles and a cute Speedo, I'm in the little pool, a middle-aged woman with sciatica and a bum knee. I felt pitifully bitter and angry. What if I didn't recover from these physical issues? Was this how I would be for the rest of my life?

The emotions were real, and I honored their voices, for a little while. Then I asked them all to please shut up, so I could try to find hope and heal. I asked for guidance and support from those who loved and guided me from the life beyond this one.

At the end of class, I limped up the pool ramp and into the locker room to change before heading home. My husband asked how it had gone. I told him I'd felt older and less healthy than the old people in the class. Knowing I love the ocean, he suggested a drive down the coast to cheer me up. I could still be a passenger in a car—all was not lost.

Cape Cod is lovely in summer, but year-rounders know its beauty in the off seasons. Steve and I drove down quiet roads, meandering through historical villages, shops, and ancient graveyards as we headed north up to Cape Cod Bay. Above snow-covered meadows, crows circled old barns and stony fields that rolled down to the frigid Atlantic.

We parked at Corporation Beach, part of a long stretch of popular sandy shoreline along the Cape's north-facing edge.

The beach was deserted and pleasingly desolate. We were surprised to see hundreds of geese and gulls hunkered down on the rocky jetty that butted against the incoming surf. Raucous gulls reeled and squawked as iron-gray breakers rolled and crested before thundering onto the jetty, where they hurled icy salt mist into the air and frozen sand. Dozens of white-feathered bodies crouched on the lee side of the jetty along the exposed tidal flats, huddled together against a stinging north wind.

A flock of brants—smallish black and white geese—shared the lee flats with the noisy gulls. The sedate brants contentedly nibbled green kelp and bobbed in the numerous shallow tidal pools left along the beach as the tide receded. I decided to get out of the car and snap some photos.

I randomly selected a brant who was busy separating a vibrant green flap of kelp from the bottom of a tidal pool. The kelp hung from his beak like a rubbery lasagna noodle. He was so earnest about his task that I laughed out loud and zoomed in the camera to get a better shot.

That's when I saw his leg. As he emerged from the tidal pool with his kelp, he dragged a grotesquely swollen, misshapen right leg behind him. He swung it out sideways as he stepped, just the way I'd learned to do to avoid the pain that bending my own knee caused.

I felt tears form as my heart reached out to the poor creature. I remembered all the poisoned robins I had tried in vain to save after the DDT trucks had done their damage. Oh, the poor hurt creatures of this world, with no one to help them!

I limped back to the truck, where Steve was keeping warm and listening to sports radio. I told him about the brant.

"What should we do?" I asked anxiously. "Do you think we should call someone? How can we help him?"

My back was to the beach as I poured out my worried questions. Meanwhile Steve was watching the brant, who was limping across the packed sand toward the open water.

"It's okay. He'll be all right. Look, he can still fly."

Sure enough, the injured brant had lifted off and was soaring over the breakers. While I was fretting over his infirmity, the plucky brant was going on with the business of living. With or without my pity, he was making his way. He could still fly.

The undeniable relevance of what was happening landed like a Hallelujah, and I honored the message as new gratitude replaced my earlier self-pity. I would be like the persevering brant, and less like the seagulls who squawked each time a cold wave hit them. Like my avian teacher, I would go about the business of my life, with pain as a sidekick if necessary. I would accept pain as a tolerated travel companion. I would honor its ability to teach me patience and mercy.

I felt the familiar goosebumps as I acknowledged the affirming connection with the Consciousphere that allowed me to interpret cosmic metaphors. I silently thanked the steadfast brant for teaching me a transformative lesson in faith. I wasn't there to save the brant; he was there to teach me. I hope that in return, my compassion eased his burden and lifted his wings.

This intuitive experience illuminated my path because my heart was open to seeing its deeper meaning. Intuition allows us see circumstances and people that offer peace, motivation, inspiration, and whatever lesson is needed. It's one of the greatest gifts opening yourself to your inner knowing has to offer.

When I sail, I monitor my position by compass, charts, and GPS. I watch for waypoints to mark correct progress along the set course. When I arrive at the numbered green can or red nun that correlates with the one on my chart, I know I'm precisely where I'm supposed to be.

That's a perfect analogy for intuitive synchronicity. Synchronicity events are the waypoints that let you know you're exactly where you're supposed to be. Once you learn to use your intuition and watch for your waypoints, you will never meander far off course again. Your aim will be true.

Once upon a time, on a brilliant summer day long ago, a young man and woman took a break from college studies to spend a day playing like kids on Mayflower Beach. They ran barefoot on the broad sandy flats on the north coast of Cape Cod Bay. They dug clams, swam in the bracingly cold north side waters, sunbathed, and laughed.

There came a moment when the young man stopped digging a sandcastle and looked up at the woman standing beside him. He grew suddenly serious. The sun made him squint as it glittered off the white sand. He covered his brow with his hand to shield the sun and see her more clearly. He looked into her eyes and with bare, honest feeling, said, "You're beautiful."

She smiled at him and turned to look across the broad expanse of water to the distant horizon. Something indescribable was happening. Something was calling to her.

A knowing came. Without words, the knowing spoke to every cell in her being. It said, "You will travel so far, only to return to this moment."

She didn't know what to make of the experience. It was far too big to grasp. The future had spoken, from someplace without a name. Years passed, but she never forgot the moment when he'd said she was beautiful, and the universe had whispered something back.

Thirty years later, after much life had passed and both were alone once more, they met again on the beach. With the same bare feeling in his voice, he said, "You're beautiful," and married her on the spot where the universe had shared its prophetic message.

**CHAPTER 20**

— ⌀ —

# Grasping the True Nature of Existence

Where is there? And what is there?
Is there a there over there?
Or is here simply everywhere?

IF DR. SEUSS had been a quantum physicist with metaphysical leanings, he might have asked these questions. The ability to receive and communicate information from "somewhere" that doesn't feel like "here" begs many questions about the nature of space and time.

Stories of people reporting near-death experiences (NDE) have become more prevalent in the media. Are more people nearly dying and rushing back to tell their stories? Maybe. We do save more people from the brink of death thanks to modern medical technology. Or has our culture softened its skeptical opinion of NDEs? Are more people coming forward because it's safer to speak up without fearing recrimination? I entered "near-death experience" into a search engine and got 5.8 million hits in a matter of seconds. If you're interested in reading scholarly articles on the topic, look on PubMed.gov, the US National Library of Medicine and National Institutes of Health website. There are nearly thirty-five thousand pages on the topic at this writing. There's an International Association for Near-Death Studies, and several *New York Times* bestsellers devoted to the topic. It looks like a lot of people are talking. That's a good sign. The first step in exploring a mysterious state of being is admitting that it exists.

Scientists refute interpretation of the visions and emotions experienced during NDEs as real events—although we can argue for chapters about what precisely defines real. They point to "brain spikes," a final burst of hyperactive electrical energy in the brain as it approaches death and frantically strives to make sense of what's happening. Some medical peers like my physician assistant friend Alfred postulate that a chain of neurochemical events creates the experience and that the chain explains why so many people see and feel the same thing: bliss, peace, beautiful light, and occasionally less pleasant experiences such as falling. The prevailing scientific view of NDEs is that they are hallucinations. Therefore, they are not proof of an afterlife, or a facet of life that includes a realm we don't typically consciously encounter in our day-to-day living.

Here's some much-needed clarification, courtesy of intuition. NDEs are neither hallucinations nor evidence of an afterlife. They're simply a window into a facet of *this* life, experienced at a different level of consciousness. There is no afterlife, because before and after are not words that apply to human existence outside of the body. There is one eternal life that simply looks and feels differently depending upon whether or not you happen to be in a body. We do not leave this life for an afterlife. We exist in an everlife.

Embracing this model of existence in no way disparages the glory of life beyond the body or the doctrine of religious belief.

If anything, mystical experiences lend credence to everlasting life because they reflect facets of its spectacular nature like surfaces of a flawless diamond.

Brain spikes at or near the moment of death don't explain the vast array of psychic visions and premonitions experienced by the dying, or the living. I'm very much alive and well when I receive messages from the other side.

We're using woefully inadequate tools when we apply pure science to questions of existence. The human mind requires intuition *and* reason to reach conclusions. It's an interdependent system, like conscious and subconscious mind states. Scientific research doesn't apply intuition, except in the beginning when someone has a flash of insight that leads to the breakthrough.

I'm not saying we shouldn't employ science as we explore the mystery of intuitive knowing, but we must be skeptical of a method that completely dismisses the influence of the observers—you know, us, the existees. It's why intuition cannot be proven through science alone. It is something that must be experienced. We help define reality, and we have intuition, so intuition is part of reality.

Werner Heisenberg and Niels Bohr's Copenhagen interpretation is a famous example of scientific method bumping up against the active role of the observer in the outcome of scientific experiments. They note the puzzling behavior of subatomic particles that appear to vary their activity based on whether or not they're observed, raising the question of whether anything is real before it's perceived. It seems our consciousness links us not just to each other, but to everything.

Likewise, Jonas Salk wondered if all of reality exists in a state of possibility until actualized by the human mind. The theory of biocentrism, put forth by Robert Lanza MD and Bob Berman, explores this concept.

Could it be that reality as we perceive it, including the glorious realm known in religious doctrine as heaven—that place on the other side of the veil—exists in an implicit state that requires specific circumstances (such as the existence of an observer, or an intuitive observer in an altered state, or the death of the body) to actualize? Consider this: If consciousness is the glue of the universe, and intuitive experience is a motherlode of expanded awareness and power, then we have unimaginable influence over our existence. Our consciousness perceives reality through different facets, depending on whether we're in human body form, in an altered state, or freed from our body and existing as pure consciousness in the Consciousphere. It's like putting on different sunglasses and seeing how the world changes. It's still one world. The lens is just different.

If all of us regularly accessed this fount of information and guidance we're all connected to, what would our world look like? I imagine there would be huge currents of creative energy released into art, medicine, politics, and humanitarian efforts. How differently would we treat one another if we accepted that intuitive knowing cannot exist unless we are a unified energetic force?

Remember those ancient world maps depicting a flat earth? At the edges, where the earth was believed to drop off into oblivion, were inscribed the words, "Here There Be Dragons." Those dragons symbolize fear of the unknown. It's instinctive to fear the unknown. The tendency serves us in an evolutionary sense. But so does our intrepid curiosity. Intuitive knowing would not have survived into the present if it did not serve an evolutionary purpose. Our mechanistic culture, increasingly detached from a grounded connection with the earth, has forgotten its inherent worth.

Intuition is simply a state of heightened consciousness, and at its core consciousness is pure love, not fearsome dragons.

Consciousness, where intuitive knowledge dwells, is an extension of our day-to-day reality. It's part of here. It's existence. Existence doesn't have a here and a there, a before or an after. That's why I can sense spirits. How could I sense them if they weren't present for me to sense?

Like the old flat-earth maps, our perception of reality is falsely limited. We don't live on a flat, existential plane with a scary drop-off point called death. Death is an illusion, like the edges of the old flat earth. Life doesn't suddenly end. Like the illusion of the line at the horizon, death is just a trick of perception. Just like our spherical mother planet, life is a sphere that flows on and extends beyond the visible horizon we call physical death. Life only appears to stop at death.

You know how you can see a ship's smoke billowing even after the ship has passed from view across the horizon? Think of life like that. Intuition is the smoke. It's proof that the SS Everlife keeps going. Mediumship and psychic knowing are proof of a truth humans have sought for as long as we've existed—everlasting life.

# The First Time My Father Died

This is the story of my father, Jack, who died twice.

Jack was a concrete thinker. He was all left brain, to use a popular but completely inaccurate phrase. He was an electrical engineer with Raytheon Corporation, an international aerospace and defense company based in Massachusetts. Dad wore thick glasses and white-collared shirts. His shirt pocket sported a white plastic pocket protector stuffed with pencils and a slide rule. I never heard him wax poetical or saw him behave in anything resembling a philosophical manner. He was a man of pure science. He loved charts and graphs, mathematics, astronomy, and order.

We had enormous solar panels in our back yard back in the 1970s because he was frugal and enjoyed being on the cutting edge of innovation. He kept careful penciled notes of the ambient water temperature, time of day, and weather conditions as he graphed the solar panels' effectiveness.

He applied this level of studied observation to all areas of life. I still have his detailed, hand-written charts of my childhood allergy symptoms. He charted them seasonally to discern probable allergens. When we filled the gas tank of the family car, we had to document data in an automobile fuel efficiency log so he could monitor the car's energy performance. Are you getting the picture? He liked *Jeopardy*, PBS specials, and the History Channel. He woke us for school whistling "Reveille." He ordered us about like Captain von Trapp in *The Sound of Music*. He was not a sentimental, philosophical sort of man who spent hours contemplating the nature of existence like his inscrutable daughter.

Now that you've gotten to know Jack, I'll tell you the story of the first time he died. It happened in the cold hours of a stormy night, during a winter that had been brutal even by New England standards.

It was Thursday, February 24, 1994. Outside, the thirteenth snowstorm of the season raged. My parents were talking quietly together as they prepared for bed. For some reason, the topic of dying entered into their conversation. They were both relatively young at the time. Dad was sixty-four, Mom five years younger. We kids were grown and gone. The house was quiet, save for the groaning north wind battering the region that evening, smattering snow and sleet against the windowpanes.

Mom was strong and healthy, blessed with Hurricane Mary's sturdy constitution. Dad was frail. He had suffered with asthma all his life, a degree of depression, and complications from an undiagnosed gluten intolerance. He was no worse or better than usual on this stormy night. Yet something, perhaps the ominous winter weather, had turned their thoughts to death.

"I hope I go first. I don't want to live without you," Mom said.

"I'll be gone long before you," Dad replied.

At around eleven o'clock, they went to bed and fell asleep holding hands, as they had done for the past thirty-seven years. At a quarter to one, Mom felt Dad jerk violently. She bolted upright and called his name—"Jack? Jack!" He didn't answer. She shook him. She groped for the nightstand and switched on the light. He wasn't breathing. She gave him two rescue breaths and pumped his chest, to no avail.

She describes what happened next:

"I heard my mother's voice clear as day in my head. She was giving me orders. 'Go downstairs. Call an ambulance. Turn on the front light.' I followed her commands. Within minutes, the ambulance arrived. I let them in, and they raced upstairs. They brought their new defibrillator—you know, the one Dad had just donated money for them to buy in memory of his friend Buddy. It was the first time they'd used it. They put the defibrillator on him and gave him a shock."

I was living one town over, home alone with my two young sons. My mother's phone call woke me at one o'clock in the morning.

"Lorri, it's Mom." Her voice was shaking. I didn't need my psychic skills to know something was horribly wrong.

"Mom, what's happened?"

"Something's happened to Dad. The ambulance was here. I tried to do CPR...Oh, Lorri, I don't know if I did it right..."

I took a deep breath.

"Mom. Was Dad breathing when they took him out?"

"No."

I was newly separated from my first husband at the time. I called him, and he agreed to make a heroic drive from the city to the suburbs in order to stay with our sons, so I could go to the hospital. I cried the entire way. The roads were treacherous, and tears blurred my vision.

"Take it easy, Pook," I heard my dad's voice say.

Oh my God. It's Dad. He's talking to me. Pook was his pet name for me. He hadn't called me that in years. Wait. He's talking to me from the other side. That means he's not here anymore. Oh no. Oh no, oh no.

A sob gripped my throat. He was gone...but I felt him here... and there....what was going on? Was he dead or alive?

"Please don't leave, Dad," I cried out, pushing the pedal down.

At the hospital, I saw my friend Mark, one of the paramedics who'd responded. Dad had no pulse when they'd arrived. His heart was in ventricular fibrillation—instead of pumping blood in a normal sinus rhythm, it was quivering uselessly. Ventricular fibrillation is bad. It's the death throes of the heart. They'd used the defibrillator, applying an electrical shock that stops the heart's quivering, giving it a chance to autocorrect. In other words, the defibrillator has to kill you first—literally stop your heart dead to give it a chance to reboot itself. The paramedics had restored Dad's heart to normal sinus rhythm, but how long had his brain been without oxygen?

When I entered the emergency department I saw my dad, unconscious on a gurney. I held his hand. He was intubated, connected to a mechanical respirator that breathed for him. Tubes ran out of his body in every direction.

Mom was by his side along with a cluster of medical staff. The respirator hissed and groaned as it forced air through his lungs. Every few moments, his fists clenched and his arms curled upward.

"Oh look, Lorri, he's fighting," my mom said.

I didn't have the heart to tell her that the clenching and stiffening movements were signs of decorticate posturing, a dangerous signal indicative of increasing pressure on the brain. I wished I didn't know that so I could feel hopeful too.

What had happened to my father?

The respirator made a jarring sound every few minutes. That was a good sign. It meant he was making sporadic attempts to breathe on his own. I sensed he was in there, fighting.

Brain images showed multiple pinpoint areas of infarction in the brain, consistent with oxygen deprivation. Dad had suffered an acute respiratory arrest. The lack of oxygen to his brain had caused it to hemorrhage, possibly causing permanent brain damage. But what had made him suddenly stop breathing? We just had to wait. He would remain in intensive care for now. Sometime around sunrise, we all went home.

The following night, I arrived at Dad's beside. Nothing had changed in his appearance, but my intuition told me to speak to him—*right now*. In the most cheerful voice I could muster, I said, "Hi, Dad!"

His eyes opened.

He seemed to be searching for me, but he couldn't fix his gaze. He was still too far away to see me.

His lips moved. Then, nothing. I called to him again, but he was back in his faraway place.

Grief is love turned inside out. I fluctuated, exhausted, between these two all-consuming emotions. I asked God to help us all get through this pain.

On Saturday, February 26, I arrived at the hospital to find Dad sitting up in bed, breathing on his own. He looked at us when we talked. He smiled and nodded when I asked if he understood what we were saying. I was filled with relief and gratitude. He wasn't speaking yet, and there was likely a long road ahead, but he was back.

Over the course of the week, Dad slowly improved. At first, he slurred his words and had motor coordination problems. It was difficult for him to get a spoon of sherbet to his mouth—most of it landed in his lap. He was disoriented, so he was restrained while seated in a bedside chair. He didn't like that one bit. He ran his fingers over the cloth restraint straps.

"Get me a knife."

"I can't get you a knife, Dad."

"Why can't I figure this out? I'm an engineer, damn it!"

Eventually his motor skills and speech improved. His doctors were convinced he'd regain his baseline functioning. When I arrived to visit on day five, he looked at me with wonder on his face.

"Pook! I shook my father's hand. But I couldn't have, could I?"

He told me in great detail about his visit with his dad and his uncle Dickie, his mother's late brother. Uncle Dickie had lived with Mom and Dad for a while after his wife passed and died shortly thereafter. Dad had arranged his funeral.

"Dickie says he likes the headstone I picked out."

Now I understood why I was hearing my father's voice as I drove to the hospital. My father had truly died and passed to the other side. It was his spirit voice I'd heard on my treacherous drive to the hospital. That feeling I'd had that he was here, but not here? It was because he *was* here and there, drifting back and forth between the veil separating physical life and spiritual life.

Two weeks later, Dad returned home with a diagnosis of sleep apnea and a new CPAP (continuous positive airway pressure) machine. A sleep study revealed he'd ceased breathing in his sleep and gone into respiratory arrest.

The following August, we celebrated his sixty-fifth birthday, but only one candle topped his cake. He declared himself one year old, at the start of a new life following his death. Every year going forward was bonus time.

After he recovered, Dad had no recollection of his time in the hospital, including his comments about visiting family on the other side. Once the rational side of his mind regained control, the experience settled into his subconscious. But he was different, gentler. Something powerful had changed. I had the kind, tender dad I had always wanted.

Thirteen years later, my father left us for the last time. I was by his side, along with my mom and sisters, as we gently ushered him to the next phase with comforting words of love. He left from the room where he'd been born, died once before, and slept hand-in-hand with his bride for nearly fifty years. I know Grampa Pete and Grandma Marianne and the rest of our people were there once again to embrace him and bring him home.

This book jumps around in time, but since I don't believe in linear time anymore, I guess that's fitting. Here's the story of my own near-death experience, four years after my dad's respiratory arrest.

It was 1992, and I was living with Ken, the man who wasn't scared off after the night in Marco Island when I predicted a meteor's blazing arrival. It didn't matter to Ken that I was psychic. It didn't matter to me that he had a spinal cord injury and couldn't walk. He was fiercely independent. He worked full-time and drove a muscle car with hand controls instead of a wheelchair van. He played competitive quad rugby—or murder ball, as it's known in Europe. We shared a deep physical, emotional, and spiritual connection that is rare in this life.

We enjoyed dining out, even though we couldn't always access the front door of a restaurant due to the absence of a ramp. Although President George H.W. Bush had signed the Americans with Disabilities Act into law four years earlier, in reality things were slow to change. We'd resigned ourselves to entering eateries through garbage-lined back alleys and up flimsy plywood ramps meant for trash transport. We didn't let this dampen our enjoyment of a romantic evening out.

One balmy late summer night, we dined locally at a favorite accessible restaurant. The sky was bathed in orange and pink as the sun set on an unseasonably warm day. We feasted on warm bread and sweet butter, followed by tender escargot and goblets of cold, crisp chardonnay. Next came shrimp scampi, sautéed to perfection over angel hair pasta. The night ended with coffee drinks smothered in whipped cream. It was deliciously decadent.

When we got home, we sat up a while to digest our amazing meal. We nodded through the eleven o'clock news, then headed off to bed. Full and happy, I fell asleep immediately.

Something's wrong. Something's very wrong. Wake up. Wake up now! A voice screamed inside my head. It was my inner voice, sounding a terrifying alarm.

I'm dying. I could actually hear my own voice saying that to me.

My eyes shot open. I was covered in a film of icy cold sweat. My heart had relocated to the inside of my stomach, where it thudded sickeningly. The room spun. I felt extremely faint.

The urge to purge gripped me. I got up and stumbled the few feet from my bedside to the small master bathroom. I turned toward the toilet.

Then I was gone.

Not gone. I was somewhere else, floating. Oh, I'm floating! Like back when I was a little kid, floating on the warm waters of

Buzzards Bay. Only there isn't any water. I'm just…floating in a sea of…bliss. There was no sound. There was no light. Oh, and wait, my body's not actually floating because I'm not in a body. I was something vast, me, but also part of an enormous force.

Waves of peace infused me. I was pure consciousness, an infinite loving presence.

Wow. Wow. Harmony. Connectedness. I remember this place. This is beautiful. I'm happy. I'm where I'm supposed to be. Everything is right. No pain. Nothing but love. I'm engulfed in love. I am complete…

Something was nudging me. Stop it. Go away.

Nudge. Nudge.

What? Oh, damn. I remember now.

I had a body down there. I was floating over my old body.

I didn't want to go back into that body. I'm going to feel really, really shitty if I get back into that thing. My body's on a bathroom floor. It's a mess.

I'll stay here.

Another unwelcome nudge. I knew I had to leave. I had to sink back down into that poor sick body. I don't want to go!

I had to go.

"Lorri?"

Floating. Don't want to hear you…

"Lorri!"

That was Ken calling to me. I'd forgotten about Ken. And my boys. I have to go back to my boys.

"Lorri!"

Okay, okay. I'm coming.

By a means I can't explain, I was lowered down from the floating position above my body. Down I went, until we reconnected, me and that seriously ill body on the bathroom tiles.

Shit.

Yup. I felt like shit, just as predicted. My right arm was resting against a heat register. It was burning. That's part of what was nudging me when I was up there in the bliss. I shifted my arm away from the heater. I was back on the cold bathroom floor, too sick and weak to get up. Ken had his wheelchair wedged into the bathroom doorway; the master bathroom was too narrow for his wheelchair to fit through. I looked up at him from the floor. He looked scared.

"Kenny. Call nine one one. And get my pants."

I might have been dying, but I'm modest. I would be fully clothed when the paramedics arrived. I started to shiver and realized I was going into shock.

Ken was so nervous that he dialed 411 by mistake. Later we would joke that he dialed 411 to get the number for 911.

He tossed me a pair of pants. I was too sick to get up, but I wiggled my toes into them and wriggled them up until they reached my hands. I tugged them the rest of the way up, rolling side to side until I was decent.

A very strong paramedic lifted my dead weight off the floor and slid me onto a gurney.

The cool night air is a healing elixir. I breathed in the scent of green living things as the paramedics rolled me out of the house and into the back of a waiting ambulance.

I drifted in and out of my body. I heard the driver say "We're bringing in a forty-year-old woman, blood pressure forty over palp."

Oh, that poor woman. I wonder who she is. She's old. And her blood pressure's so low…she's a goner.

"Stay with us, Lorri," said the paramedic shaking my arm.

I spent three days in the hospital, hooked up to monitors. Vials of blood and a bunch of tests later, I was discharged without a diagnosis. But I had something better. I had proof of the everlife.

The doctors didn't know why I had nearly died, but I diagnosed myself using my trusty intuition. I began to have a recurring vision of myself curing my body by standing at a sink, humming contentedly as I rinsed my poor inflamed intestines under cool running water before tucking them back into place.

Years later, following several more hospitalizations and negative tests, I demanded to be checked for celiac disease. I just had a feeling. Sure enough, a gluten intolerance was wreaking havoc in my gut. By then I'd undergone surgery to remove a portion of damaged intestine and nearly died. My intestines literally needed to be cleansed of an intolerable protein. My doctors hadn't figured that out. Test after test had been negative. I'd been told it was "nerves" making me sick. I was nervous, all right. I was nervous that my doctors weren't up to par! Thank goodness I listened to my inner voice. If I hadn't, I'm convinced I would be dead by now.

I spent a great deal of time contemplating my near-death experience, and that of my father. Was a death hormone, a chemical manufactured by oxygen-starved tissue, responsible for my dad's experience visiting with his departed relatives, and my unconscious state of floating in a sea of perfect bliss? No. Here's the science to back me up:

My blood pressure wasn't high enough to pump adequate amounts of blood into my brain to retain consciousness. That means there was a grossly insufficient amount of oxygen circulating through my brain. My dad was also unconscious, but more deeply, in a coma state. An unconscious, oxygen-deprived brain can't create lucid thoughts and store them in long-term memory. It may fire random images and messages, but not a beautifully choreographed experience. Had I been hooked up to an electroencephalogram (EEG), it would have recorded brain activity, as had my dad's. But that is not an indication of lucid awareness.

While unconscious, I was fully aware that I was in an altered state, in a physical location that was not my body. Similarly, my dad was adamantly insistent that his visit with his deceased relatives was a real versus dreamed experience.

So, if my dad and I weren't using our brains to think lucid thoughts, what were we using? We were using collective consciousness, which exists outside of the body and does not require a brain to be. In my bliss state, I was in the Consciousphere. My unique self didn't disappear. I still felt like me. But I also felt like everything. I was me, inside a giant "we." My body was probably making brain waves. A vestigial cord of consciousness tethered me to my body, perhaps. The rest of me was experiencing my connection to a larger self. Similarly, my dad was in a coma tethered to life, but he was also with his departed family in a state of existence we don't fully understand.

Do you see what this suggests? We rock on. We are simply channeling consciousness that doesn't originate inside of us. We're distinctly unique particles of consciousness, each with our own sense of self, yet also part of a unified whole. Our bodies contain us, but they are not us. They're place cards. Eventually, when our bodies die, we just shed them and float into our higher self, which is boundless love.

Since I didn't die, I don't know what would have happened next, if anything at all. I didn't see the bright light some people report, or a departed loved one. All I know is that I was ecstatically blissful and that parting from that state was a sweet sorrow. I'm happy I remember the experience. It enlightens the way I live my life. I hope it brings you comfort. It's what is waiting, and it's beautiful.

**C H A P T E R   2 1**

# Altered States and How to Reach Them

You exist in time, but you belong to eternity.
You are a penetration of eternity into the
world of time—you are deathless, living
in a body of death. Your consciousness
knows no death, no birth. It is only your
body that is born and dies—but you are not
aware of your consciousness—you are not
conscious of your consciousness—and that
is the whole art of meditation—becoming
conscious of consciousness itself.

—OSHO

THE BEST PART of meditation is that you get to reach an altered state of consciousness without having to nearly die to get there. I've done the near-dying thing, and I've meditated my way to that same blissful place. I strongly prefer meditation.

I attended my first meditation class at the Pleasant Health Collaborative, led by my friend Nirtana Gloria Deckro.

Lying on the carpeted floor of her serene office suite, I and a small group of fellow students followed Gloria's soft-spoken prompts as she led us into a deep state of relaxation.

I'd failed to meditate "right" in the past. In my twenties, I bought a cassette tape, turned down the lights in my living room, and pushed "play." A soothing voice told me to focus on a burning candle flame and let all other thoughts come and go, but my hyperactive brain refused to settle down. In fact, it rebelled:

What if I can't stop thinking? Oops, that's a thought. I'm thinking, and I'm not supposed to be...okay, back to the tape...breathe deep, flex and relax my shoulders...oh damn...now he's moved on to the hands...squeeze, relax...breathe...I can feel my heart beating...oops...now it's beating faster because I'm screwing up... I'm a meditation failure...hey—did I leave the curling iron on?

I approached meditation like I approached life—as an all-or-nothing challenge I had better perfect, or else.

Gloria taught me there's no success or failure. This monkey mind of mine could be tamed. In her meditation class, my mind responded to her soothing words. As my body and mind quieted, something inside me released and fell away. As soon as it did, something unexpected surfaced.

I saw and felt my connection to what I now know to be the Consciousphere. I drifted in a field of all-encompassing, pulsing energy. I was aware of my body in its deeply meditative state, down there on the carpeted floor. But I was simultaneously floating in a sea of consciousness, connected to everything and everyone. I was tethered to my body by luminous bands of light that swayed gently down from my out-of-body self, like tendrils of kelp in an ocean current. I saw the tendrils of light emanating from the other students' bodies, too, connecting them to the sea of energy in which we floated.

I grew a little nervous. I was way up in the amazing oneness of the Consciousphere, but I wanted to be darn sure I could get back down there to my body, and I didn't know how to do that. I looked down. Yup, there we all were, on Gloria's rug with our energy tendrils floating upward to our ethereal selves.

"Woah," I thought. I didn't expect this. Is this what everyone sees when they meditate? Right about then, Gloria's voice shepherded us back, and like a sheep from the field, I followed her into the folds of awareness of my body, my breath, and finally, into awareness of the room around me, the floor beneath. I felt the carpet pressing against my back and opened my eyes.

I was awed—and confused. What was that place? It wasn't as vivid as my near-death trip had been, but it was every bit as real. How could I integrate this element of reality into my rational framework of what's considered real? There was literally nothing in my day-to-day life that felt connected to this. I still had a lot to learn.

I lingered after class to share my floating experience with Gloria. As she patiently listened, I saw from her expression that my description was not unfamiliar.

Students of meditation are often alarmed during their first encounter with out-of-body consciousness, but many have documented this experience. The Greek historian Plutarch wrote, "When a man is initiated into the mysteries of the beyond the soul, he has the same experience of leaving the body as it has at the time of death."

Sant Kirpal Singh, an Indian spiritual master who lived between 1894 and 1974 talked about experiencing consciousness outside of the body. He calls it "above body consciousness."

In a talk given in London in 1972, Sant Kirpal Singh said:

"So to know God we will have to know ourselves first. Like knows the like. But, unfortunately, our soul is environed by mind and outgoing faculties. Our soul is under the control of mind, mind is under control of the outgoing faculties, and outgoing faculties are dragged like anything by the outer enjoyments. So all masters said that we should know ourselves first. Know thyself! East and West makes no matter, you see. Those who have known God, they say the same thing. To know ourselves, we will have to know it not at the level of feelings or drawing inferences, but by self-analysis, by rising above body consciousness. How to? The outgoing faculties will have to be controlled, mind to be stilled and intellect also to be ceased for a while after understanding what is what. Only then we can know ourselves."

Singh understood that in order to fully know ourselves, we can't just use our intellect and our traditional senses. In fact, those things get in the way, just as they initially impeded my quest to understand my own gift. Control of "the outgoing faculties" (our senses) is possible when we're dreaming, or in meditative states, or in a near-death experience. Those are portal states—thin places.

Wise humans have been writing about consciousness and higher awareness for centuries. Like I said, I arrived late to this party. You have too. That's okay. We made it. We're here, so let's talk some more about intuition, enjoy the appetizers, and meet some new people.

**C H A P T E R   2 2**

# Interviews

WHAT'S IT LIKE to live with an ability that's not widely accepted or respected in professional circles? The responses I received are remarkably consistent. Lisa's answers are representative of the sample:

How comfortable are you with your abilities?

Very. I enjoy when I can find time to nurture them, as the more I get caught up living in my head, the more they dwindle.

Can you/do you freely share your talent, or is it something you feel you must hide?

I more often hide than share. Most of the world looks at you with a question mark, wondering if you're really all there, if you share such experiences.

With what percentage of your friends are you able to reveal your abilities?

With one hundred percent of my true friends; those who I don't share with are not really my friends.

If you're uncomfortable sharing your talent, what is it that prevents you from doing so?

The judgments and being considered crazy

What do you believe is the nature of psychic ability? Why are we able to know things without the use of our five senses? What do you think explains why intuition happens?

I think we all have the ability. Some just live so much in their heads, they forget that they are energy and part of something more. I think our vibrational senses tie us into a stronger knowing, and some are just more open to tapping into it.

Being considered crazy is a ubiquitous—and rational—concern of most respondents. Beth, the woman whose dead boyfriend visited her condo and caused her dog to go on high alert, shared two more experiences. Both were prefaced with the ubiquitous prediction of being labeled crazy. That vein of fear runs deep. Even an intuitive writer exploring intuition and requesting stories is suspect:

You're going to think I'm crazy after you read all of this. But you asked, so here goes. About a week before my dad passed away, I had one of those dreams where it was incredibly real, where the people in the dream were truly there.

I was sitting in a room surrounded by all the female members of my family who had passed away:

grandmothers, my aunt, cousins, etc. They were telling me that it was time for my dad to cross over but not to worry...they would take very good care of him. I woke up in a cold sweat.

So, the following Sunday, I'm supposed to be driving out to New York. My sister was out there, at the hospital with my dad. He was not well, and we knew that.

I kept trying to get my car packed up and get on the road, but bizarre things kept happening to hold me up. For example, there was a piece of glass in my bed—yes, really! It sliced the side of my foot, and I couldn't get it to stop bleeding so I could shower and get ready to go. Then, a long-lost friend called out of the blue... Finally, at about 1:00 p.m., I'm driving down my driveway...it was one of those odd November-weather days. I noticed black and purple clouds over the field across the street with biblical-looking rays of sun breaking through the clouds. At that moment, a song that I'd never heard before was on the radio; I can't remember the name, but it is a man recounting his life. At that point, I said out loud to myself, 'Dad just passed away...' I arrived at the hospital three hours later to be met by my sister and brother. They told me Dad passed at about 1:00 p.m. They hadn't wanted to call me while I was driving.

In my more than thirty years of nursing, I encountered many stories like Beth's. Look at the obstacles placed in Beth's path to her dying father's bedside: a deep wound that took a long time to stop bleeding (precisely the way we experience grief). A long-lost friend reaching out across the distance (a perfect symbol of everlasting connection despite separation).

Often, dying people wait until their children arrive, or until they've left, before they pass. This is intentional. Some people don't want their loved ones' last physical memory to be of them leaving. Instead, they choose the Irish goodbye (where one slips away from a party without farewells so as not to make a fuss).

# Back to Beth

This past February, I released my very first real-estate listing. The following morning was crazy with people calling for showings, etc. Quite the wild ride. In the early afternoon, I stretched out on my couch to just close my eyes for a few...

I'd been up late, and up early. It would have been my twenty-fifth wedding anniversary, had I still been married. So I was doing a little of that congratulatory thinking, recognizing how far I'd come. From there my mind drifted to how relaxing it was to be able to take a catnap, thinking about how my father had come home for lunch almost every day and took a nap before returning to work, and I was truly understanding why he did it. As I lay there, I got a really strong sense of the energy of another person in the room. I could feel the energy and understand that it was near my TV and doorway into the living room. I opened my eyes and realized that it was my dad; he was standing there, telling me I should be proud and that I'd done a good job. Yep, I cried.

Okay, last one. A month or so after the visitation from my dad, I was driving down the highway, thinking about my confusion with my current relationship, sorting the good and the not-so-good. Suddenly, my mother was in my head as clear as if she was sitting next to me (she used to give killer dating advice) and she says, 'He really loves you, you know.' I swear I almost drove off the road…

Now that you think that I am totally off my rocker…I did at one point meet a professional psychic at a function. So I asked her, when people are so incredibly real in a dream, are they really there, is it a visitation or just a really vivid dream? She explained that if people on the other side want to reach out, they usually do it through our dreams because our subconscious isn't immediately saying 'oh, this is crazy' and just discounting it. She told me that when I felt an energy to recognize it, talk to it. Because they like it when we recognize them and will then try to reach out more often.

What have I learned from all of this? There are no co-incidences. Songs on the radio that remind you of things, feelings of energy, feathers, cardinals, etc.?

Nothing is coincidental.

I agree with Beth. Will there be people who make spurious correlations between personal experiences and random events? Of course. Reason must not be discarded like the proverbial baby with the bathwater. I don't believe that every time a hapless bird flies into my house, it means a death is imminent, like my Scottish grandmother Hurricane Mary MacLeod had. Superstition and intuition are different creatures—although they've probably dated in the past.

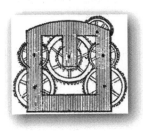

# CHAPTER 23

⸙

# Rethinking Time

I'VE HELD OFF on tackling the time conundrum until now because I wanted you to get to know me before throwing linear time up for reconsideration. It's time to take another look at the linear progression of time and the presumed order of past, present, and future.

We've explored intuition, channeling, and near-death experiences, all of which occur naturally as part of the human experience. We've seen how these experiences logically suggest we're all connected via an encompassing energy field aka Consciousphere that allows information to flow freely between us. Our separateness is therefore an illusion, propagated by the fact that we presently inhabit distinct physical bodies. We've seen how consciousness survives physical death, cruising on blissfully into a new state of being in the everlife. On these things we are seemingly in agreement since you're still here. So let's explore the concept of time.

Reviewing the evidence, we frame the following statements:

1. People who have experienced physical death and are presumably no longer "here" are able to communicate through receptive mediums.

2. It is occasionally possible to accurately predict future events such as deaths, injuries and celestial events.

These events made themselves known before they manifested in material form. Here are some possible explanations for accurate precognition by human beings:

a) It is fake news.
b) A hormone did it. It's a biochemically mediated hallucination.
c) It's all explained by simple coincidence.
d) A neurobiological misfire in the brain causes a temporary lapse, which leads to a false perception of reversed time flow.
e) There is some kind of magic going on.
f) Time as we perceive it doesn't exist.

I'm going with (f). There are books dedicated to explaining how time is a tool we use to name and organize a sequence of moments, but it is not an actual thing. Would there be something tangible called time if no human was measuring it? Nope. There would just be now. It's the tree-falling-in-the-forest conundrum. If ears and brains aren't interpreting vibrations moving through air into noise, is there a sound? Nope. There is only the potential for sound if an entity with fully operational ears and a brain is present. The same thing goes for time. If a human isn't around to remember and catalog a series of now moments, is there time? No, there is not.

If a future event can be known in the present, then the event is not entirely in the future, is it? It has a foot in the now. Or maybe the other foot, and the rest of its body too. So time is not tidily flowing from past to present to future. It's an illusion of our biology. The sharpest living minds of our species are busy sorting out this puzzle. I'm not a genius, regrettably, although my permanent school record does apparently have that impressive abstract-reasoning capacity documented somewhere. I'm just a curiously intuitive medium, noticing odd little blips here and there in the flow of reality, like Neo in *The Matrix*. Time theories abound. When it gets dizzying, I default to my intuitive knowing. It smiles patiently and tells me time is a handy tool, not an actual property.

Whether we understand it fully or not, empirical data suggests that our concept of time cracks under closer scrutiny. It works well for organizing our days and getting us to appointments at predictable moments, but it doesn't jibe on the cosmic scale. Consider for a moment that time and space are tools we use, not actual conditions existing outside of the brain. The implication is that reality looks a whole lot different when you're not looking out through a body.

This isn't something we need to fret about right now. I just want you to be aware that this quirkiness about time is another hint offered up by intuition that we aren't getting things exactly right. The universe is crackling with mysteries, just waiting for our wits to sharpen.

**CHAPTER 24**

# How to Attract Butterflies

JOCELYN, A FELLOW intuitive woman, once explained mediumship to me this way:

"Spirits are like moths, Lorri. And your porch light is on. They see the light, and they fly to it. You can't turn off your light. You can ignore the moths, but they're not going away, so you may as well acknowledge them."

She was right about not being able to turn off my light. I had tried throwing figurative rags over it before, but the rags caught fire and left me with an even bigger mess on my hands. I'm a gardener, so instead of moths, I'll share a butterfly garden analogy to help you learn how to attract spiritual abundance. If you want to attract butterflies, you cultivate a garden filled with their favorite plants for feeding and breeding. You may see the occasional butterfly flit through your yard without a butterfly garden, but if you plant specifically to entice them, you're pretty much guaranteed.

So how to prepare your spirit garden? Here are tips from a master medium gardener: First, create harmony and order in your living space. Decluttering your surroundings will instantly help you to feel calmer and free your energy. Order and harmony will generate a sense of calm. Calmness is your fertile soil. Your eyes need a place to rest in your daily environment. Grab a book on fêng shui, and get busy weeding your yard to make room for the crop.

Practice mindfulness. Long walks in nature accomplish this for me. Some people practice yoga. I get regular massages to quiet my busy mind and hypervigilant muscles and to allow energy to flow more freely through my tissues. You may bring your mind into the peaceful present through movement or through listening to soothing music. Being in the presence of pets, plants, and happy people is a good way to quiet your mind and focus it on the present. Traditional meditation is certainly a tried and true method. Mindfulness is your clean, pure air.

Invite connection. Ask the universe to bring you a greater sense of connectedness with consciousness. Say it out loud, with feeling. It may feel a little odd. Do it anyway. Ask for dreams and serendipitous signs. It may take time to see results. Germination is a process. You are asking for your seeds.

Let yourself experience love. Hug babies if you have any around. Laugh. Read poetry. Sing. Pray. Have lunch with an old friend. Marvel at a sunset, a new green leaf, or a work of art. Take time to allow the simple pleasure of these things to fill your heart. This is how you water your garden.

Play. When I was a school nurse, a little girl invited me to go skipping with her. I hadn't skipped in a really long time, like maybe half a century. I wasn't sure I could still do it. But you know what? I could. I skipped down an entire corridor and back again. The principal looked at me funny, but that's okay. People might look at you funny too. Skip anyway. If you can't skip, find another way to play. Play is sun for your garden.

Our wise friend Osho speaks of the value of play. He writes:

Take hold of your own life. See that the whole existence is celebrating.

These trees are not serious; these birds are not serious. The rivers and the oceans are wild, and everywhere there is fun, everywhere there is joy and delight.

Watch existence, listen to the existence, and become part of it.

Patience, Grasshopper. While you're waiting for your garden to grow, hang out with intuitive people and ride the slipstream of their energetic connectedness. It works. It's like playing tennis or golf with a better partner. Practice noticing how you feel around certain people, preferably strangers with whom you don't have established emotional history. Coffee shops and restaurants are good places to practice. Notice how you feel when you look at a certain person. Warm? Wary? What can you imagine about them? Where do they live? What do they like to do? We unconsciously pick up lots of clues from others. You won't be able to corroborate your impressions without coming off like a weirdo stalker, so don't worry about that right now. Just practice. Rumi said, "There is a voice that doesn't use words. Listen." Just listen.

If you're an academic type, you may want to take a course or two. Be sure to research the presenters and the school. Read online reviews. Don't overpay. You can learn a lot of what you need to know by talking with other intuitive women. Most of us are happy to talk about our abilities with a genuinely interested person.

Now your garden is ready. Welcome the butterflies.

# CHAPTER 25

—⚭—

# Semantics of Acceptance

MY FRIEND DAVID responded to my request for psychic interviewees by writing,

"I don't have intuition, but I have a strong gut instinct about people." The term "gut instinct" is a culturally acceptable man-phrase for intuition. This got me thinking about how semantics impede the effort to reclaim the power of intuitive knowing. The terms "metaphysics," "intuition," and "psychic" still readily conjure up crystal balls, tarot cards, and carnies. As a practitioner of holistic health and therapeutic massage, I encountered the same problem when I opened my doors. For years, the tawdry term "massage parlor" was applied to establishments offering access to the world's oldest profession. Massage suffers guilt by association.

The terminology we use to define intuition is in need of re-framing. The list of synonyms offered in a thesaurus is sparse—instinct, presentiment, premonition, inkling, idea, sense, notion... none of these seem to adequately capture its scale. Using words to define something boundless and ineffable is a tricky business.

I'm drawn to "prescience," not least because of the amusing play on words: intuition certainly existed pre-science. Whatever words you choose to use, always use them with authority—and never, ever in the same sentence as the c-word.

**CHAPTER 26**

—∾—

# Can Intuition Alter Human Evolution?

AS A SPECIES, we carry forward traits that have proven successful to our survival. Intuition is one of those traits. It's critical for our survival, like our ability to reason.

Jonas Salk saw intuition and reason for what they are—two elements designed to function in dynamic interaction. He understood that the fundamental unifying principle in the cosmos is relationship. He noticed that a pattern of relationship duality exists in all of nature. For example, a cell exists in relationship to its host, the body. We are individuals, interrelated by our species. Our cosmos is rife with examples of yin-yang relationships. The human mind possesses a functional relationship between reason and intuition, which we've been downplaying for about two centuries.

Underused components atrophy and eventually disappear from the gene pool. It's why our tails disappeared as we evolved and stopped living in trees. Vestigial tails are still present in human embryos up to around thirty-five days' gestation. Will intuition suffer the same fate if we continue to ignore its relevance in human evolution? Unlike tails, intuition remains a useful tool in the modern age. Global communication has never been easier thanks to technology, but has human connection kept pace? Diplomacy is more important than ever as we wrestle with profound cultural divides. Trade, commerce, global stability, and scientific advancement all depend upon our ability to respectfully communicate with one another. In other words, our evolution hinges on our ability to master interconnectedness.

Salk writes: "We are at an important juncture in human evolution, and even, one might say, in cosmic evolution. The role of reason and intuition in the process of knowing, of knowing what is right and wrong in terms of what is evolutionarily right and wrong. The merging of intuition and reason will provide wisdom for the resolution of the struggle in which we are engaged."

What does evolution have to do with the way we think? More than you think!

If you subscribe to the belief that we must all be connected, otherwise intuition and psychic knowing would be impossible, then it follows that our thoughts affect each other. This alone lends credence to the power of prayer, whether or not you believe in a deity. Our thoughts matter. Salk writes: "Most human beings do not see themselves, or their minds, as serving the process of evolution. Nevertheless, it would represent a major phase change in the evolution of human consciousness for such a realization to occur and to be acted upon. At this point in our evolution, as we further cultivate the human mind, we are becoming more and more aware of the role and the importance of intuition and reason in human evolution as well as in everyday life."

It's important for Salk's words, published in 1983, to survive and resonate in our culture today. Salk ardently believed that the ills of the human predicament can be repaired through the reconciliation of the intuitive and reasoning abilities of humanity. He imagines, as I do, an increasingly complex human mind evolving through *volitional intent* as we actively adapt our thinking to apply reason and intuition to our fundamental understanding of the cosmos. We must engage in conscious evolution. Science can only take us so far.

Scientific method led us to profound discoveries about our universe, but until we put ourselves back into the equation, our way will not be clear. The Bible says God made man in his own image. This is an important symbolic clue. We must look within for the ultimate answers to existence and our own survival as a species. Salk asks us:

> "What is our duty in the light of our trusteeship in the process of evolution? If we trust evolution, we must learn to trust ourselves, our intuition and reason. We can feel as well as know; we can know intuitively as well as cognitively. There is more than one way of knowing. We must use all the many ways of knowing. We can know subconsciously in sleep and in wakefulness. We can know with or without words. We can know with or without science. But we can know more with language and with science than without them."

**CHAPTER 27**

꧜

# Bringing it Home

She decided to free herself, dance into the
wind, create a new language. And birds
fluttered around her, writing "yes" in the sky.

—MONIQUE DUVAL

FREEDOM LOOKS DIFFERENT to each of us, depending on where we begin. We all have personal confines to break as we reunite with intuition. If you are shy, intuition will break open your voice. If you struggle to be taken seriously, intuition will infuse you with unshakeable confidence. If you feel isolated, sad, or alone in this world, intuition will remind you that you are deeply loved and never truly alone.

How will you choose to use your intuition to guide your life? If you're not sure, the beauty is that you can ask the Consciousphere for guidance and know that your request is heard and guidance will come. Like most profound truths, it's that simple.

I spent this past Christmas at my childhood home, where family had gathered to break bread, recollect old times, and celebrate life. I'd finished the final draft of my manuscript and mailed it off to my editor for dissection. I was feeling good about my efforts and anxious to spend time relaxing in the company of family, past and present.

I pulled into the drive and was struck by the realization that for over a century, my ancestors have lived, loved, worked, argued, laughed, and celebrated together in this house. My mother is the last of the line. When she leaves us, hopefully many long healthy years from now, our house will welcome a new family. Do our spirit relatives depart when we do, replaced by new guardians of the living? I wonder how my own human story will end, where my spirit will gravitate when my body returns to the earth. I believe we follow our loved ones, wherever they may be.

It's been ten years since my dad died. Mom sleeps alone in the old house now. Well, probably not, but she can't sense the spirits the way I do. As the house fills with returning family and the aroma of turkey and pumpkin pie, I stand alone in the kitchen, looking out over the silent, wintry gardens and snowy fields. I recall happy childhood days when the yard was full of life—kids playing, birds singing, flowers blooming. All of us present, alive, together.

Now the yard is still, darkening as daylight wanes. The pines along the perimeter wear a mantle of snow on their boughs. I stare at the empty birdbath near the garden wall I helped my father build. A rim of ice glitters in the bowl, reflecting the last rays of sun. I allow myself a moment of wistfulness as I gaze at the frozen, empty lawn, longing for those now passed.

A spirit voice says, "We are but two seasons of one beautiful garden. There is nothing to fear."

As often happens when the veil drops away, goosebumps course over my skin—the body's acknowledgment of spiritual communion. I feel the profound solace of interconnectedness. Our garden is truly everlasting.

These are the gifts of intuition: the ability to feel love from those who have departed from us in physical form, attentiveness to the spiritual needs of others, the comforting knowledge that we are never alone, the ability to see synchronicity and allow it to guide our life path. There are signs everywhere, waiting for our wits to sharpen.

"Mom, look at this. It happened just before you got here."

My son is gesturing for me to look at his smartphone. He shows me a photo of a strikingly large red-tailed hawk, in full winter color. Its majestic body dwarfs the frozen bird bath where it stands, haloed in clear light, staring directly into the house.

# Afterword

I HOPE THIS exploration of intuition has been enlightening. I hope it inspires you to lift intuition out of the shadow of reason, its boisterous fraternal twin, and let it stand proud.

Speak often, openly, and unapologetically of how intuition informs your path. Lead others by your bold example. Jonas Salk discovered the polio vaccine by using his intuition to imagine himself behaving as a virus would: "I would picture myself as a virus, or as a cancer cell, for example, and try to sense what it would be like to be either. I would also imagine myself as the immune system, and I would try to reconstruct what I would do as an immune system engaged in combating a virus or cancer cell."

He admitted to this, and he still had friends.

# Acknowledgments

WITH GRATITUDE TO my husband, Steve, who married me on Mayflower Beach thirty years after destiny whispered my truth. His love and enthusiastic support give me courage to attempt great things. I'm indebted to my clever sister Mary for her unfailing encouragement and expert editing, as well as for her fashion advice, which keeps me from looking like a reclusive hermit. Thank you to my soul sister Terry Jane England for her wonderful crow cover art. Thanks are due to my friend Beth Johnson of E. T. Johnson and Associates for cheerfully helping me wrestle the manuscript into submission-ready form. Special thanks to Beth Manhardt, LICSW, for her insightful clinical reflections as I nurtured this most personal of projects. I'm grateful to my mother, Gyneth, who normalized my intuitive abilities during times when they worried me greatly. I am humbled and blessed by the loving guidance of my ancestors, who light my path and visit at just the right times. Finally, to all who shared their stories, thank you for your courage.

# About the Author

Lᴏʀʀɪ Aɴɴ Dᴇᴠʟɪɴ, RN, BSN, MS, is a clinical research manager and a registered nurse. She holds a master's degree in metaphysics and founded and operated a national biotech and pharmaceutical consulting firm.

Devlin brings her analytical background to her study of psychic abilities. She understands the fear many women share about revealing their psychic abilities in the modern world and hopes to encourage and inspire readers to listen to their intuition and explore their abilities.

Devlin has been published in medical and pharmaceutical trade journals, online blogs, and magazines. She is also the author of the children's book *Cape Cod Critters: A Fun Look at Cape Cod Wildlife.* She lives on Cape Cod with her husband Steve and has embraced her gift as a psychic medium and spiritual teacher.

# Notes

## Rights and Permissions

Excerpts from Jonas Salk, *Anatomy of Reality: Merging of Intuition and Reason*, reprinted with permission of Columbia University Press via Copyright Clearance Center.

Ruth Nanda Anshen's biographical excerpt is used with permission of the Jewish Women's Archive, Brookline, MA. https://jwa.org/people/anshen-ruth/

Sant Kirpal Singh quotes used with permission of Unity of Man, Austria/Europe, www.kirpalsingh-teachings.org. His lectures and writing from which quotes were used can be found on this website.

Osho quotes used with permission of Osho International.

Available from Amazon.com, CreateSpace.com, and other retail outlets.

46436060R00113

Made in the USA
Middletown, DE
31 July 2017